50 HIKES

IN COASTAL AND INLAND

50 HIKES
IN COASTAL AND INLAND MAINE

FIFTH EDITION

John Gibson

THE COUNTRYMAN PRESS

A division of W. W. Norton & Company

Independent Publishers Since 1923

For information about permission to reproduce selections from this book,
write to Permissions, The Countryman Press,
500 Fifth Avenue, New York, NY 10110

For information about special discounts for bulk purchases, please contact
W. W. Norton Special Sales at specialsales@wwnorton.com or 800-233-4830

Manufacturing by Versa Press
Book design by Chris Welch

Library of Congress Cataloging-in-Publication Data

Names: Gibson, John, 1940-
Title: 50 hikes in coastal and inland Maine / John Gibson.
Description: Fifth Edition. | Woodstock, VT : The Countryman Press A division
of W.W. Norton & Company, [2016] | Series: 50 Hikes | Title varies: 2nd
edition published as: 50 hikes in southern and coastal Maine; 3rd edition
published as: 50 hikes in coastal and southern Maine; 4th edition
published as: 50 hikes in coastal and inland Maine. | Includes index.
Identifiers: LCCN 2015048516 | ISBN 9781581573572 (paperback)
Subjects: LCSH: Hiking—Maine—Guidebooks. | Maine—Guidebooks.
Classification: LCC GV199.42.M2 G54 2016 | DDC 796.510974104—dc23
LC record available at http://lccn.loc.gov/2015048516

The Countryman Press
www.countrymanpress.com

A division of W. W. Norton & Company
500 Fifth Avenue, New York, NY 10110
www.wwnorton.com

1 2 3 4 5 6 7 8 9 0

Remembering Bessie Hanson Gibson and John Edward Gibson,

who introduced me to the Maine woods at a tender age.

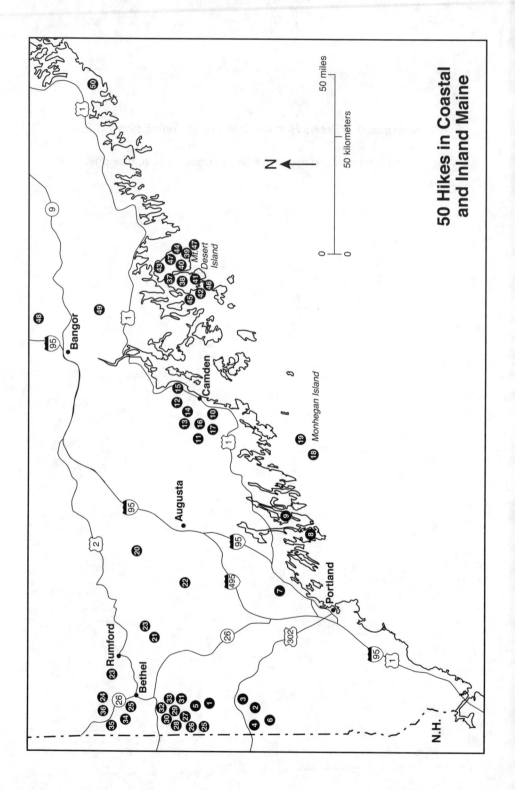

50 Hikes in Coastal
and Inland Maine

Contents

Introduction

Welcome to the pages of this 40th Anniversary Edition of *50 Hikes in Coastal and Inland Maine*. This illustrated guide has been updated to provide hikers with complete and current information on many of Maine's best hiking destinations. New hikes have been added—maps and directions updated where needed—with new photographs of trail features throughout. Trail extensions, relocations, and improvements are included in hike descriptions, and clear trail maps on USGS overlays are provided with each hike. Detailed driving directions to each trailhead will guide you easily to trail destinations.

You'll find 50 exceptional hikes described in detail in these pages. In selecting hikes to be included here, our emphasis has been on coastal and upland destinations that are interesting to walk, beautiful to see, and reflective of the environmental richness of the Maine landscape. Trail descriptions include information on hazards where present, and in the section to follow are suggestions about what to carry, packs, footwear, clothing, and other useful information. Comments on the history, geology, forestation, flora, and fauna of the terrain you'll hike are here, too. In short, you'll find everything you need in this volume to make your hiking days enjoyable, interesting, and enriching.

Maine is northeastern America's great hiking state, a place of mountains large and small, oceanside ranges "where the mountains come down to the sea," as Edna St. Vincent Millay wrote, and many inland ranges that offer exceptional backcountry walks in an unchanged landscape. Maine trail organizations, land preservation groups, and government agencies are working to hold the line against unwise development and to add new acreage to protected lands. Regional trusts have become the framework of preservation for some outstanding new hiking sites now open to the public, especially in coastal and riverine lands. Expanded hiking opportunities have been created in areas such as the midcoast and its connected backcountry, central Maine, and Maine's western mountain region. Opportunities for hiking in Acadia National Park and on Maine's offshore islands have grown, too. (See also the author's *Enjoying Maine's Islands* and *Walking the Maine Coast*, both published by Down East Books in 2005 and 1991, respectively.) This guide directs hikers to both long-established trails and newer hiking opportunities.

Despite renewed interest in promoting new trails and protecting Maine lands from despoliation, the pressure to, as Joni Mitchell sings, pave "paradise to put up a parking lot" is present in Maine as elsewhere. It remains important that hikers and people who generally enjoy Maine's outdoors make their voices heard against sprawl and destruction. The Maine backcountry, wherever situated, has come under assault from developmental pressures, road building, mining, overuse, resort building, and aggressive timber harvesting. A report entitled "Patterns of

COASTAL HIKERS OPPOSITE GOGGINS ISLAND

Change," commissioned by the Maine Land Use Regulation Commission, has illustrated that about half of all development in Maine in the last 40 years has been in previously wild areas, particularly the fabled North Woods. The Natural Resources Council of Maine called the situation "wilderness sprawl." If you value unspoiled countryside in which to hike, camp, fish, hunt, or cross-country ski, please support the conservation organizations that are working to keep Maine green. Work in your community to implement and apply reasonable protections against the damaging sprawl that is gobbling up open countryside. Make your voice heard.

This 40th Anniversary edition of *50 Hikes in Coastal and Inland Maine* will guide you along trails on the Maine Coast, extending from Maine's border peaks in the southwest to the highlands of Evans Notch and the Mahoosucs, and to the gentler summits of the Oxford Hills and Central Maine's lakes region. This volume is not meant to send you to every obscure nook and cranny, of which there are hundreds in Maine's backcountry, but to guide you to appealing walks in areas of unspoiled, natural beauty where a refreshing hiking experience is accessible and rewarding.

Regardless of hiking ability, experience, and inclination, you will find many hikes here that offer delight and challenge. In the headings for each hike you'll find information that will help you select those hikes most appropriate for you. The distance to be walked, the amount of elevation to be gained, and the approximate time needed for unhurried completion of each hike is noted. The maps, commentary, and travel directions in this guide will get you there and back safely.

WITH MAP AND COMPASS

Many individuals who are just getting acquainted with hiking enter the woods without map-reading or compass skills. The information in this volume will go a long way to keep you going in the right direction. Still, knowing how to use a map and compass will add greatly to your sense of well-being and safety in the woods wherever you walk. If you would like to develop good map and compass skills, try *Be Expert with Map and Compass* by Björn Kjellström (Wiley, 2009), an excellent introduction and skill-builder. Introducing children to hiking with a map and compass will add to their sense of adventure and confidence in the woods—a life-long benefit.

The hikes described in this guide may be situated near settled areas, others are in rural backcountry, while some lie in established parklands. Most paths are well-marked with signage and paint blazes on trees and ledges. Some hikes noted here may not be blazed completely, or have had signage and markings disappear due to weathering over time. Experienced hikers are familiar with this challenge, but if you are not, the maps and trail commentary in this guide become very important.

Carry this volume with you in your pack and consult it regularly, as needed. The maps and trail directions offered here are adequate for most hikers to complete each hike comfortably and confidently. Carrying a compass will allow you to orient yourself to the landscape through which you are walking and to maintain your direction of travel with help from the trail comments in these pages, which give frequent compass directions. For those who prefer it, carrying USGS maps that show the wider terrain through which you'll hike will help provide a better sense of the lay of the land and its features. Increasingly, these maps can be obtained online (see: www.usgs.gov/pubprod). There are useful Maine area maps developed by the Appalachian Mountain Club, often available in mountain shops, sporting goods stores, and bookstores, that cover some of the hiking venues noted in these pages. In some concentrated Maine hiking areas, local hiking groups have developed maps. For Evans Notch, for example, the Chatham Trails Association, a hiking club, has developed excellent local charts. The routes shown in maps in this guide appear as overlays on USGS charts, so there is no need to purchase extra maps unless you prefer to have them.

The modern assumption that "I don't have to worry if I get lost, I'll just call for rescue on my cell phone," is widespread. It is also badly mistaken and irresponsible. Much of Maine hiking is sufficiently remote that there may be no agency close by that can quickly come and get you. In some rural areas cell phone reception is spotty or nonexistent. Organizing a rescue costs money for already overtaxed services. Pulling Fish and Game wardens and police personnel from regular duty to hunt for a lost hiker wastes official resources. Getting lost and rescued might cost you plenty, too. In some states, irresponsible behavior by lost hikers requiring a rescue can lead to the hiker being billed for the cost of the search and rescue, a fine often in the thousands. New Hampshire already has such a law; Maine is considering similar legislation. The solution is simple: Keep this guide with you, use its maps and route descriptions, carry a compass, and stay on the trail. You'll do just fine.

Some who enter the woods without a guide such as this believe carrying a GPS device will reliably point the way. This, too, is not necessarily true. As with cell phones, access to a signal may be spotty or absent. Mountainous terrain can create strange, interrupted signal effects. GPS batteries can fail when most needed. An Appalachian Mountain Club magazine, *AMC Outdoors*, compares the compass-and-map route finding versus use of GPS devices; the results show that the GPS devices provided incorrect information or interrupted communication periodically. If you know how to use it, a compass always works. It needs no batteries, nor satellite signal—magnetic north never takes a day off.

CLOTHING AND FOOTWEAR

Today, outdoor clothing meets the needs of hikers more completely and reliably than ever before. The old saying "cotton kills" remains true, however. Cotton clothing, especially outerwear, is an unwise choice for a day in the woods and hills. New synthetic fabrics that, unlike cotton, do not absorb and hold moisture, are used today in wind and rain shells, shorts, pants, and shirts. These will keep you dryer, warmer, and safer. Cotton clothing, wet from perspiration, rain, or snow, chills the body dangerously at higher, exposed elevations. Cotton clothing is also difficult to dry out once wet. In the colder seasons, dry clothing is essential for comfort and safety.

For a half-day or day-long outing on the trails described here, a long-sleeved shirt, shorts or pants, a wool sweater, and wind and rain shell are plenty. An extra shirt and second pair of wool socks provide comfort if the ones you're wearing get damp or wet. On mountain walks, especially in spring and autumn,

ON THE BALD ROCK MOUNTAIN TRAIL (SEE HIKE 15)

put a wool sweater, hat, and gloves in your pack. When choosing clothing items for hiking, buy those that are all or at least part-synthetic. Well-made, breathable synthetic garments resist wear, don't hold moisture, and dry quicker. Always err on the side of carrying a bit more warm clothing than you think you'll need. Remember, too, that, even on sunny, dry days, wind chill at higher elevations may leave you cold and uncomfortable. A light wind shell or anorak will be worth many times its weight in preventing heat loss. The use of new synthetics also has resulted in lighter weight clothing, as found in the new fleece garments that offer both warmth, quick drying, and extreme light weight.

Selecting appropriate footwear for hiking should be a rational process, but often it isn't. Many prefer to set out on a hike in sneakers or running shoes, neither of which is a good choice. They're not waterproof, and neither provides solid support or protection against rough and rocky trail surfaces. Battering your feet

walking on rocks and ledges, even on a shorter hike, makes no sense. On many of the longer, higher hikes in this book, good, sturdy hiking boots with lug soles are essential. They provide real support, protect ankles and toes, absorb impact, grip slippery, wet rocks better, keep your feet dry on wet ground, and resist torsional twisting. Lowa, Vasque, Danner, L.L.Bean, EMS, and REI offer a variety of boots suitable for the trail. Well-made, Vibram-soled boots with leather uppers are far superior to the cloth hiking shoes and boots marketed today. Be especially suspicious of molded plastic synthetic soles made in Asia. Bargain-basement boots with injection-molded soles usually can't be re-soled. A welted, quality leather hiking boot costs more, but, kept waterproof and taken care of properly, will last you over 20 years with occasional re-soling if required. Shop carefully and avoid bargain-basement boots that will likely fall apart just when you need them most. In the woods and hills, your boots are your transportation system.

PEMAQUID POINT LIGHT

OVERNIGHTERS AND SHELTER

There are several hikes in this volume that can become overnighters, stopping about mid-way to camp if you wish. Staying the night on the ridges begs for some sort of shelter in case the weather catches up with you. Ultralight tentage for one or two persons is available from Sierra Designs, Kelty, L.L.Bean, Marmot, MSR, EMS, and REI. If you're hiking alone, a bivy sack will protect you from the elements at an even lighter weight. (L.L.Bean's Microlight FS1 is probably the lightest 1-person tent available at 2 pounds, 11 ounces.) For most warm-weather camping a light-weight, mummy-style sleeping bag with synthetic fill is sufficient. Choose a bag good to 30 degrees, and carry a shorter-length sleeping pad.

For those who love to carry a bigger pack and to get away for a couple of days or longer, the possible overnighters described in this book are: Hike 5, Miles Notch–Great Brook Loop; Hike 15, Bald Rock Mountain Loop; Hike 27, Conant Trail; Hike 32, Caribou Mountain Loop; Hike 31, Albany Mountain, (camping at the US Forest Service [USFS] site at Crocker Pond); Hike 34, Mount Carlo–Goose Eye Loop (camping at Carlo Col Shelter site); Hike 50, Cutler Coastal Trail (camping at Fairy Head campsite). Some of these campsites do not allow fires. Any cooking should be done with small, portable backpacking stoves that use white gas or butane. Always carry out what you carried in. Some of the trails described here cross or run over private lands. Please respect the landscape and leave it undisrupted and cleaner than you found it.

DRINKING WATER

Small-stream pollution is still rare in Maine, but especially near settled areas, it's wise to boil or disinfect your water—or carry in your own safe water. Streams flowing in fields where there are cattle are particularly suspect. Much has been written in the way of warnings about Giardia recently.

These are naturally occurring parasites, frequently transmitted by beavers as well as humans, that may occasionally be found in mountain streams and ponds. They cause a most unpleasant affliction, as the parasitic cysts fasten themselves to the stomach lining and cause nausea, cramps, diarrhea, and transient feverish symptoms. It would, however, take an awful lot of heavily infested water passing through your body to create the likelihood of a really bad case of giardiasis. Still, it's wisest to get your water from a reliable spring; or, if you must use stream water, choose a fast-moving stream and then boil, disinfect, or filter it. Better still, fill your water bottle back home or at a known safe water site whenever possible.

HIKING WITH CHILDREN

Hiking is a great experience for children and an excellent family activity. The pastime can foster in children an appreciation of the woods and conservation that will endure for a lifetime. Hiking too far with children who are too young is a different story. Most of the trails in this book can be navigated by children who are at least five or six years of age. Where terrain is difficult or severe, the text so indicates, and such trails are probably not good family choices to pursue with youngsters.

Kids don't have the endurance of adults, and little legs have to work harder on the trail, so plenty of thought should be given to distance as well as elevation. Attempting hikes of 2 or more miles with children who are only three or four years old usually is much too taxing and will result in a spoiled trip for everyone, with tired, cranky youngsters who have to be carried a good part of the way. Parents should use sound judgment in carefully estimating the hiking ability of their youngsters and not push young children into long, forced marches beyond their ability. The purpose of being in the woods is for all, young and old, to enjoy themselves, right?

Involving kids in plant, tree, and landmark identification can boost their enjoyment of any hike. Informal instruction in the use of a compass and map reading will also help them trace their route and prepare them for safe hiking later, on their own. A backpack well stocked with interesting snacks and beverages will help combat the fatigue factor, too.

TRAIL DIRECTIONS AND ELEVATIONS

As suggested earlier, always carry this guide with you as you hike so that trail descriptions and maps are readily available. Carry a compass and follow trail directions if in doubt. Keep in mind that actual elevation gained may be greater than the posted height of a mountain, as some trails descend and then climb again several times as you progress. The suggested hiking time for each route is based on a comfortable walking time, not a mad dash. Some hikers will find they can complete hikes in less time than suggested, and others will require more. Find a pace comfortable for you that allows you to see and enjoy the natural features of the terrain through which you're walking. Hiking isn't a contest. Remember, too, there are many summits on which you'll want to linger, enjoying the view and the Maine air. Finally, let someone know where you're going and approximately when you expect to return. Good hiking!

Hikes at a Glance

Hike Name	City/Town/County/Region	Distance (in miles)	Difficulty
1. Sabattus Mountain Loop	Southwestern Maine	1.8	Easy
2. Mount Cutler, Hiram	Southwestern Maine	2.5	Moderate
3. Pleasant Mountain, Bridgton, and Denmark	Southwestern Maine	3.5	Moderate
4. Burnt Meadow Mountain Loop, Brownfield	Southwestern Maine	3.25	Moderate
5. Miles Notch Loop, Stoneham	Southwestern Maine	11	More Difficult
6. Peary Mountain, Brownville	Southwestern Maine	2	Easy
7. Bradbury Mountain Loop, Pownal	South Coast and Camden Hills	3.75	Moderate
8. Ovens Mouth, Boothbay	South Coast and Camden Hills	3.5	Moderate
9. Dodge Point Circuit, Damariscotta	South Coast and Camden Hills	2.5	Easy
10. Mount Battie, Camden	South Coast and Camden Hills	2	Short and Stee
11. Spruce Mountain, South Hope, Rockport	South Coast and Camden Hills	4.2	Moderate
12. Cameron Mountain, Lincolnville, and Camden	South Coast and Camden Hills	6.3	Moderate
13. Maiden Cliffs, Camden	South Coast and Camden Hills	2.25	Moderate
14. Ocean Lookout Loop, Mount Megunticook, Camden	South Coast and Camden Hills	2.7	Moderate
15. Bald Rock Mountain Loop, Lincolnville, and Camden	South Coast and Camden Hills	3.5	Moderate
16. Ragged Mountain, Camden	South Coast and Camden Hills	3	Moderate
17. Bald Mountain, Camden	South Coast and Camden Hills	2	Moderate
18. Monhegan South Loop	Monhegan Island	2	Easy
19. Monhegan North Loop	Monhegan Island	2	Easy

(All distances are round trip or around loop)

Rise (in feet)	Views	Waterfalls	Good for Families/Kids	Notes
500	*		*	Open views from high ledges, loop
800	*		*	180-degree summit views, wooded approach, views into New Hampshire's White Mountains
1,500	*		*	Southern ledges, open, grassy summit, tower, broad western views
1,145	*		No	Broad southern views, open summit, ledgy approach, access to Stone Mountain, loop
2,150	*	Seasonal	No	Splendid, long, backcountry ridgewalk, rough camping possible, descent via Great Brook
500	*		*	Shorter, easy hike with westward summit views to NH, eastward views over Brownfield Bog and Saco River Valley
200	*		*	Loop, beautiful hemlock forest, coastal view, camping available
260	*		*	Moderate hike, close-up river views, unique history, exceptional walk on varied terrain
230	*		*	Red pine forest loop, Damariscotta River views, eagles, ospreys
600	*		*	Woods and mountain walk, water views, mountain views
500	*		*	Shorter attractive hike to two summits with ocean and inland views
700	*		No	Easy, quiet, woods walk, old tote road, western views
700	*		*	Bold cliffs, splendid water and mountain views, short and steep ascent
850	*		No	Moderate hike, outstanding ocean and island views, park woodlands, loop, camping available
800	*		*	Moderate hike, fine water and ocean views, open summit ledges
850	*		*	Moderate hike, fine water and ocean views, open summit ledges
780	*		*	Meandering short, steep trail to ocean views, open ledge, cross-island return
150	*		*	Shore walk, cliff walk, stunning ocean views loop
100	*		*	Cathedral Woods, cliff walk, stunning ocean views, cross-island return, loop

Hike Name	City/Town/County/Region	Distance (in miles)	Difficulty
20. Round Top Mountain, Rome	Central Region and Oxford Hills	4.5	Moderate
21. Black Mountain, Sumner	Central Region and Oxford Hills	3.5	More Difficult
22. Mount Pisgah Loop, Winthrop and Wayne	Central Region and Oxford Hills	2.1	Easy
23. Bald and Speckled Mountains, Woodstock and West Peru	Central Region and Oxford Hills	4	Moderate
24. Rumford Whitecap, Rumford Point	Central Region and Oxford Hills	4	Moderate
25. Mount Will Loop, Newry	Central Region and Oxford Hills	3.3	Moderate
26. Deer Hill, Stow	Evans Notch and Region	4	Moderate
27. Conant Trail Circuit, Stow	Evans Notch and Region	5.5	More Difficult
28. Ames, Speckled Mountains–Blueberry Ridge Loop, Stoneham	Evans Notch and Region	8.25	More Difficult
29. East Royce Mountain, Batchelders Grant Township	Evans Notch and Region	3	Moderate but Steep
30. Blueberry Mountain, Stone House–White Cairn Loop, Stoneham	Evans Notch and Region	4.25	More Difficult
31. Albany Mountain, Albany Township	Evans Notch and Region	3.8	More Difficult
32. Caribou Mountain Loop, Batchelders Grant Township	Evans Notch and Region	7	Difficult
33. The Roost, Batchelders Grant Township	Evans Notch and Region	1.7	Easy
34. Mount Carlo-Goose Eye Mountain Loop, Riley Township	Mahoosuc Region	7.8	Difficult

Rise (in feet)	Views	Waterfalls	Good for Families/Kids	Notes
640	*		*	Longer woods walk, tote roads, easy grades, lake and mountain views
1,250	*		No	Backcountry woodland hike, southern summit views, obscure trail, timber yards, summit ledge
450	*		*	Summit fire tower, varied forestation, views to Atlantic coast and to NH's White Mountains
1,500	*		No	Two summits, outstanding views, some steeper sections, summit ledges
1,550	*		*	Moderate grades, extensive open ledges, excellent summit views over Androscoggin River Valley, mountain views
1,100	*		*	Limited northern views, ledgy, steep descent, outstanding views from southern ledges, loop
1,250	*	River Rapids	*	Multiple mountain and valley outlooks, ledgy, stream crossing, loop, camping available
1,200	*		No	Deep woods circuit over several low summits, fine northern views, abandoned farmsite, gem mine, lake views, steep section
2,150	*	Yes	No	Long, gradual ascent, former tote road, summit views over Caribou Wilderness, return on open ledge with excellent views
1,700	*		*	A short, steep scramble to excellent notch views, brook crossings, open ledgy summit
1,400	*		*	Wooded loop to Blueberry Mountain ledges, steep descent with outstanding views
1,100	*		No	Wooded hike to extensive, ledgy summit, multiple outlooks with fine views, many brook crossings, bog
1,900	*	Yes	No	Wilderness hike, wide summit ledges, splendid summit views, stream crossings, moose country
440	*	River Rapids	*	A short, easy hike to high ledges with valley views above the Swift River, loop with road return, camping available
1,800	*		No	Long loop over two major summits with outstanding views, Success Pond Road access

Hike Name	City/Town/County/Region	Distance (in miles)	Difficulty
35. Old Speck, Grafton Notch	Mahoosuc Region	7.5	Difficult
36. Table Rock, Baldpate Mountain, Grafton Notch	Mahoosuc Region	2.8	Moderate to Difficult
37. Pemetic Mountain, Mount Desert Island	Mount Desert Island and Acadia National Park	2.5	Moderate
38. Parkman Mountain and Bald Peak, Mount Desert Island	Mount Desert Island and Acadia National Park	2.5	Easy to Moderate
39. Gorham and Champlain Mountains, Mount Desert Island	Mount Desert Island and Acadia National Park	6	Moderate
40. Penobscot and Sargent Mountains, Mount Desert Island	Mount Desert Island and Acadia National Park	5	Moderate
41. Norumbega Mountain, Mount Desert Island	Mount Desert Island and Acadia National Park	2.75	Easy
42. Acadia Mountain Loop, Mount Desert Island	Mount Desert Island and Acadia National Park	2.5	Easy
43. Cadillac Mountain, South Ridge, Mount Desert Island	Mount Desert Island and Acadia National Park	7	Moderate
44. Sand Beach and Great Head, Mount Desert Island	Mount Desert Island and Acadia National Park	2	Easy
45. The Bubbles, Mount Desert Island	Mount Desert Island and Acadia National Park	3.5	Moderate
46. Beech Mountain, Mount Desert Island	Mount Desert Island and Acadia National Park	3.5	Moderate
47. Saint Sauveur–Flying Mountain Loop	Mount Desert Island and Acadia National Park	6	Moderate
48. Sunkhaze Meadows National Wildlife Refuge, Milford	Mount Desert Island and Acadia National Park	2.5	Easy
49. Great Pond Mountain, Orland	Mount Desert Island and Acadia National Park	4.25	Moderate
50. Black Point Brook Loop, Cutler Coastal Trail, Cutler	Mount Desert Island and Acadia National Park	5.8	Difficult

Rise (in feet)	Views	Waterfalls	Good for Families/Kids	Notes
2,730	*		No	An often steep, wooded climb to one of Maine's highest summits, tower views over Grafton and Mahoosuc Notches
900	*		*	Appalachian Trail hike to splendid views of Grafton Notch, Old Speck, and other mountains, alternate cliff ascent
950	*		*	Easy trail, fine woodlands, summit ledges offer excellent views northward
700	*		*	Interesting, short, varied trail to two low summits with views over Upper Hadlock Pond
1,200	*		*	Fine ridgeline hike with bold ocean views
1,150	*		*	Ladders, ledge, broad Acadia-wide views, sea views to Cranberry Isles
600	*		*	Straightforward, easy hike to low summit with mid-island views west of Lower Hadlock Pond
500	*		*	Easy route over open summit with excellent views over Somes Sound, return via woods road and Man O' War Brook
1,230	*		No	Outstanding sea views from open ledges in all directions, gradual ascent to Cadillac summit, views to Cranberry Isles, 360-degree summit views
200	*		*	Easy loop in southeast quarter of Acadia with views over Frenchman Bay and Newport Cove
800	*		*	Interesting circuit over two, symmetrical mountains with views over Jordan Pond and Eagle Lake
700	*		*	Woodsy loop in the southwest corner of Acadia above Beech Cliff and Canada Cliff, water views over Echo Lake, tower
1,100	*		*	Extended walk above Somes Sound over four low summits, returning by Man O' War Brook road
50 (+/-)	No		*	Easy walk through preserved wildlands, bogs, stream, cedar swamp, avian and animal species, boardwalk
800	*		*	Woods walk to broad summit ledges with superb views of surrounding uplands and Penobscot Bay
400	*		*	Stunning oceanside cliff walk and loop above Maine's "Bold Coast," limited camping on trail extension at Fairy Head

I.

SOUTHWESTERN MAINE

Sabattus Mountain

DISTANCE (ROUND TRIP): 1.8 miles	
HIKING TIME: 1 hour, 45 minutes	
VERTICAL RISE: 500 feet	
MAP: USGS 7.5′ North Waterford, ME	

For a rise of modest proportions, Sabattus Mountain offers hikers rewards unexpected on a 1,253-foot elevation. It confirms the old adage that "good things come in small packages." Sabattus lies in Lovell in the heart of Maine's western mountain country, a place of lakes, foothills, and easily accessible trails. The mountain rests in a 177-acre preserve of state-owned land and features a newly constructed loop through attractive, mixed-growth woodlands that provide an inviting half-day hike. Once a "straight up and straight back" trail, the newer loop here is somewhat longer than the original route and more interesting. The improved trail and preservation of this land is the result of a cooperative effort between the Maine Bureau of Parks and Lands, the highly successful Land for Maine's Future program, and the Greater Lovell Land Trust.

Getting to the trailhead is straightforward. From the intersection of ME 5 and ME 93 (Main Street) in Lovell, drive north on ME 5 to Center Lovell, pass the town offices, and shortly bear right (east) on Sabattus Road. In 1.5 miles, go right on Sabattus Trail Road (gravel), and follow it uphill three-quarters of a mile. The trailhead and parking area are found on the right, just past the Willoby place.

The trail begins at the southwest corner of the parking area, enters stands of hardwoods, and almost immediately reaches a junction. Turn left and southwest here, and ascend gradually in young growth regenerating after an apparent cut several years ago. Silver birches, ash, and beech are seen. The trail widens slightly and runs over a seasonal brook, pulling more around to the southeast. Threads of bright green lycopodium border the path, and, if you look carefully, there are signs of old logging

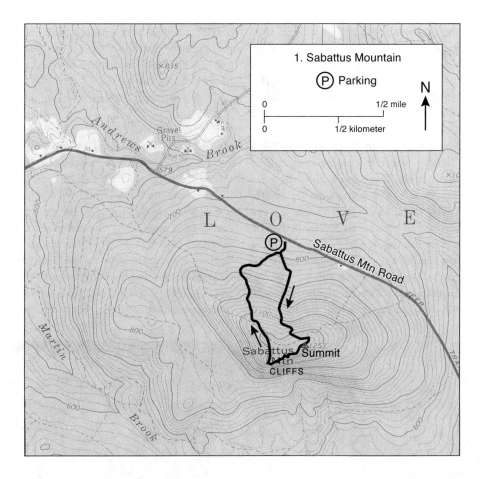

roads across the mountainside. A shallow ravine appears to the left, and the trail next ascends more steeply south-southwest up a rib of higher ground in a corridor of spindly white pines and scattered white paper birch. In some places the trail has acted as a conduit for rain and snowmelt, and there are some washouts. In the colder months, when the leaves are off the trees here, a glance back over your shoulder yields a view of hills to the north.

You climb steadily as the path enters stands of hemlock and red spruce with trailside patches of sphagnum moss. The trail continues its rise, levels off briefly, and leans to the southeast through a couple of bends. The route is more sheltered now in a fine grove of tall hemlocks and occasional red spruce—these conifers now mostly replace the young hardwoods so conspicuous below. You next walk a short distance nearly eastward as the grade eases. Patches of exposed ledge appear, and, in a few minutes, you bear right and walk onto the summit dome, following the ledge with emerging views to the south and southwest. In a few dozen yards the old footings for the long-removed Maine Forest Service fire tower lie to the right. Continue along the ledge to the southwest as splendid views open up to the south, southwest, and west.

The summit ledge here allows room

for moseying about, but use caution, especially with children, as the ledge drops off precipitously. The excellent views range from southeast to northwest, taking in the imposing mass of Pleasant Mountain in Bridgton, which lies well to the south beyond Kezar Pond. More to the right stands North Conway, where the prominent drumlin that houses Cathedral and Whitehorse ledges is visible. The lengthy north-south expanse of Kezar Lake is seen in the foreground to the west. Northwest from the end of the summit rock are views of the nearby mountains of Evans Notch. Beyond, the bold 6,288-foot summit of New Hampshire's Mount Washington can be seen on a clear day.

Sabattus forms as a fine platform for taking in the uplands of western Maine and eastern New Hampshire as you are likely to find anywhere.

On the ledges you are at the midpoint in this walk, and will find the return half of the loop just north of and behind the former tower footings. Hike northward and northwest now, descending in mixed growth as the path follows a long-disused tote road. The exposed ledge of the summit yields now to a leaf-strewn route under more hemlocks and pines as you drop rapidly north and northwest. Summit vegetation gives way quickly to clusters of young hardwoods such as you passed on the ascent. Sabattus is not a high mountain, but it definitely has vary-

VIEW FROM SABATTUS MOUNTAIN

SNOWY SUMMIT OF MOUNT WASHINGTON

ing climatic zones, as the change in the type of tree cover illustrates.

The trail levels off periodically and then continues to drop north-northwest. Roughly 0.6 miles below the summit, the route makes an abrupt right turn away from the old roadbed you've been on and drops steadily to the northeast over damp ground. Continue to the northeast here as the path levels off on another old roadbed. Continuing in this direc- tion, you shortly reach the trail junction where this hike began, and, just beyond, the parking area.

Sabattus is an inviting hike any time of year, and mountain views are quite spectacular during foliage sea- son. Those who are familiar with snow- shoeing on hilly terrain will find this loop a challenging and attractive walk in winter. Snowshoes equipped with crampons should be used.

Mount Cutler

DISTANCE (ROUND TRIP): 2.25 miles

HIKING TIME: 2 hours, 20 minutes

VERTICAL RISE: 800 feet

MAP: USGS 7.5' Cornish and Hiram, ME

West of Sebago Lake and rising above the banks of the Saco River, Mount Cutler in Hiram provides pleasant day-hiking in the quiet hill country of southwestern Maine. This rangy hogback with its pronounced southern ledges delivers excellent views for a mountain of modest height. Cutler offers a platform from which to view surrounding hills to the north, south, and east, plus New Hampshire's nearby White Mountains to the northwest. The village of Hiram is a quiet country crossroads in an attractive Maine region, free from the crowds and summer bustle of those towns eastward around Sebago.

Several trails ascend Mount Cutler. The hike described here climbs from the mountain's north side on the North Trail, and then joins the Barnes trail as it follows the mountain's ridgeline, drift-

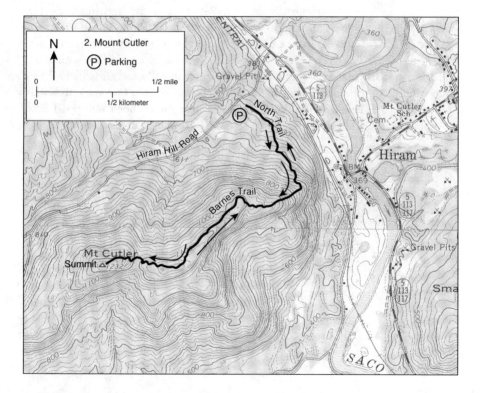

THE VIEW FROM MOUNT CUTLER'S SUMMIT

ing southwest and west to the summit. To reach the trailhead, drive northwest on ME 113 and ME 5 from an intersection with ME 117 on the west banks of the Saco River in the center of Hiram. A half mile above the bridge, turn left on Hiram Hill Road, going over an abandoned rail line. You'll find the trailhead on the left (south) side of Hiram Hill Road a short distance after crossing the tracks at two blue-blazed white pines. Park here.

Hike south and southeast on the North Trail in mixed-growth wood-lands, dominated by pines. Ascending on moderate grades, you pass the White Flag Trail connector on your left at 0.25 mile from the road. Soon the path climbs steeper ground and saws its way upward in pretty groves of lofty eastern hemlock. At the top of this steep section the trail leads to an open, ledgy plateau. Here there are views to the northwest and north of Burnt Meadow and Pleasant Mountains (see hikes 4 and 3). Continue upward as the trail climbs through stands of mixed hardwoods and then over more ledge.

Watch for a stone cairn where you reach a junction with the Barnes Trail at .5 miles. There are limited views over Hiram here, also.

Turn right and southwest on the Barnes Trail. This path, probably the original on this mountain, skirts the edge of a high tableland above Cutler's abrupt, south face. Walking southwest toward Cutler's high point, you rise gradually through a series of openings with periodic views to the south, east, and northwest. One of the rewards of this route is that you are seldom far from an outlook over the surrounding Saco River Valley countryside. The trail follows the 1,000-foot contour line and then gains another hundred feet as it proceeds southwest. You walk over a dome and then drop slightly to a spot where signs of an old tote road appear. The steep Saco Ridge Trail comes in from the southeast here. Continue southwest a short distance, rising to Cutler's 1,232-foot summit and its fine views to the south, southeast, and east. This is a comfortable place to rest, regroup, and eat lunch before heading down.

The return is made by retracing your earlier steps along Cutler's ridgeline on the Barnes Trail for 0.6 miles to the North Trail cairn. Turn left and north there, dropping down Cutler's north slope to the point on Hiram Hill Road where you began this hike.

Pleasant Mountain

DISTANCE (ROUND TRIP): 3.5 miles

HIKING TIME: 3 hours

VERTICAL RISE: 1,500 feet

MAP: USGS 7.5' Pleasant Mountain, ME

Pleasant Mountain is an impressive, rangy peak that rises dramatically west of Moose Pond in Bridgton and Denmark. The north end of the mountain contains a ski area, but the rest of this big peak remains forested and unspoiled.

On US 302, drive about 4 miles north and west from the center of Bridgton to the road that serves the ski area on the mountain's northeast slope. Take Mountain Road (the first left off US 302 after you pass Moose Pond) and watch for trail signs just over 3 miles south of US 302. A new parking shoulder has been built on the east side of the road. Make sure your car is fully off the road and not blocking traffic when you park.

The Ledges Trail, sometimes called the Moose Trail, begins its ascent from the east side of the mountain along the route of a gravel fire road. Paint blazes mark the route for its entire length. You walk first northwest and west up the broad fire road, passing through patches of wild raspberries. Shortly the road narrows to a trail eroded by water. Climbing steadily west and southwest, you reach a fork in the road (which is again wider at this point). Bear left here, and—as you make an easy arc more toward the southwest—cross two small brooks in an area thickly grown up with young birch, beech, and cherry.

You then begin the steeper climb up to the ledges as you wind west up the ridge. The trail in this section suffered a lot of damage from winter blowdowns in an ice storm in early 1998, and there still may be short sections that go around blocked areas. At just under 1 mile, you climb over outcrops of Chatham granite that indicate the beginning of the ledges. Soon you move up out of the trees and merge onto the ledges proper.

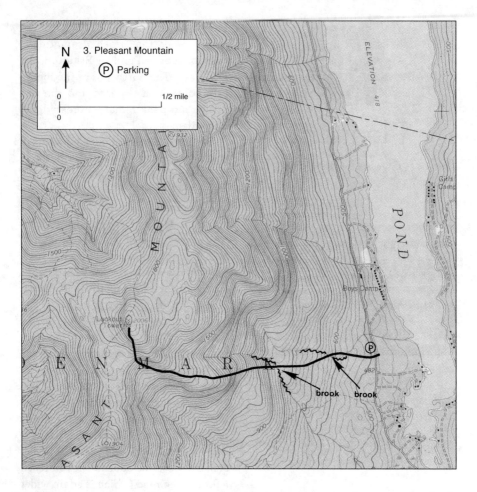

N

3. Pleasant Mountain

Ⓟ Parking

0   1/2 mile

0

There are fine views here to the southwest, south, and to the southeast over Moose Pond. Continue by climbing gradually around to the northwest, with the southwest hump of the mountain becoming visible through the young oaks along the trail. Painted trillium grow in the shallow topsoil.

You soon pass over a second open ledge area with good views to the west and southwest. Meandering first northeast and then northwest again, you climb more steeply over ground covered with low-bush blueberries, scramble over more ledge, and pass a third open ledge, which looks off to

the west. Turn northeast again, climb over an outcrop, and then turn north. In a few yards you'll reach the summit and fire tower on a grassy lawn that was once the site of the Pleasant Mountain House. The summit house was reached via a carriage road which comes in from the north

The views to the west and northwest from the "Green Pinnacle" are spectacular on a clear day. The Presidentials in New Hampshire stretch north to south on the distant horizon. Carter Dome is clearly visible over the west tongue of Pleasant. Tiny Kezar Pond and the narrow thread of Kezar Lake lie to the northwest, while Lovell Pond near Fryeburg can be seen to the southwest. The fire tower, abandoned by the State of Maine, is not staffed, and the ladder has been partially removed. If you arrive on the summit on a sunny summer day, you will be tempted to spend a leisurely hour or two, resting on the grass and ledge here.

To descend, retrace your steps for a brisk downward hike of about 50 minutes.

VIEWS TO THE SOUTHWEST FROM THE SUMMIT OF PLEASANT MOUNTAIN

Burnt Meadow Mountain Loop

DISTANCE (ROUND TRIP): 3.25 miles

HIKING TIME: 3 hours

VERTICAL RISE: 1,145 feet

MAP: USGS 7′ Brownfield, ME

As the northernmost peak of the Burnt Meadow Range, this 1,575-foot mountain lies like a great, half-risen loaf of bread south of Brownfield center. Burnt Meadow, with its sister peak Stone Mountain and three, unnamed summits, provides an excellent outlook over a dozen other hills in west-central Maine, close to the New Hampshire border. There are also limited seasonal views toward New Hampshire and the Presidential Range. The trail network here has been enlarged and improved in recent years thanks to the AMC and Friends of Burnt Meadow Mountain volunteer efforts. Plans call for an eventual connection between these summits and trails on Mount Cutler to the south (see Hike 2).

A major fire occurred on Burnt Meadow in 1977, accounting for its younger, mainly deciduous forestation. The burn, removing ground cover and duff, left considerable exposed ledge on the southeast side of the mountain. Today, resurgent hardwood cover on this and surrounding uplands makes this particularly inviting hiking terrain in the autumn foliage season.

Burnt Meadow is reached by driving to the junction of ME 113 and ME 160 in Brownfield. Go west on 160 through the village for about a mile, and make a sharp left opposite the community church. Follow 160 south, passing a cemetery and, on your left, attractive Burnt Meadow Pond. Once past the pond, watch on your right for a signed parking area and trail board for Burnt Meadow Mountain, 3 miles south of Brownfield village.

From the trailhead here, hike west and southwest on moderate grades through hardwood and white pine cover bordered with ground juniper. The trail winds upward over occasional exposed stone, with mica schist and quartzite

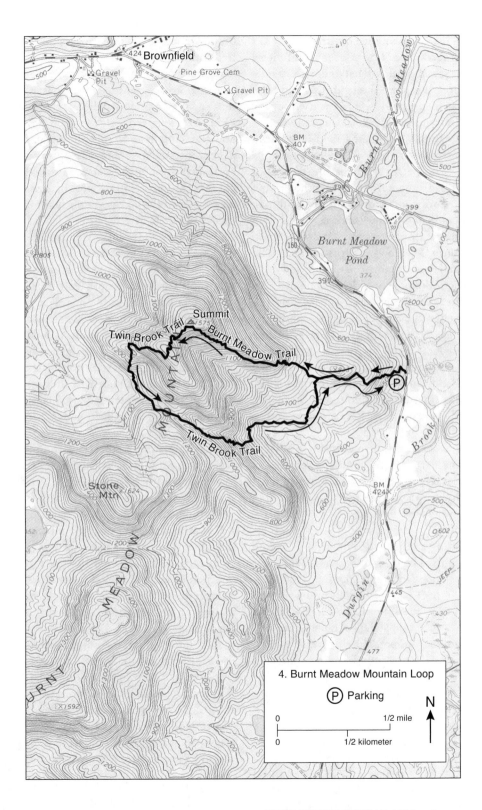

424 Brownfield

Pine Grove Cem

Gravel Pit

Gravel Pit

BM 407

BM 407

Burnt Meadow Pond

160

391

374

399

Summit

Twin Brook Trail

Burnt Meadow Trail

Twin Brook Trail

Stone Mtn

Brook

Durgin

BM 424

602

445

JEEP

477

430

4. Burnt Meadow Mountain Loop

Ⓟ Parking

N

| 0 | | 1/2 mile |
| 0 | | 1/2 kilometer |

veins visible in the host granite. Breaks in forest cover offer occasional views east and south. At just under a half mile from the road, the trail dips and then reaches a point where the Twin Brook Trail enters left. You will come to this junction again via the Twin Brook Trail on the return part of this loop.

The path rises steadily now as it pulls to the north and then northwest in hardwood groves where white oak and beech grow. Views begin to open up and the cover thins out as you climb Burnt Meadow's southeast arm. The trail crosses more open ledge and additional expansive views appear. Staghorn sumac and red spruce line the route as you arrive at an open bluff. You walk to the north next in mixed hardwoods where bearberry, goldenrod, and ground blueberries grow profusely along the path. Walk through a small clearing, working your way around to the northwest. At the 800-foot contour line, the grade steepens considerably as you continue northwest above a deepening ravine to your left. Mountain ash, hemlock, red spruce, white pine, and sumac surround a small clearing, and, ahead now, you can see lines of tilted, layered rock you'll soon scramble over. The ledge underfoot is dotted in places with weathered lichen. After a minor drop amid spindly hardwoods, the trail ascends again and opens to further views to the south. Dwarf oak grows amid patches of blueberries and ground juniper. Here and there windbeaten pines stand against currents from the southwest. Besides smaller, transient bird species, you'll likely see ravens (*Corvus corax principalis*) floating on upcurrents as you approach the summit, speaking to one another in their familiar *quorking* sounds.

A final push over ribs of fractured granite ledge brings you on to the partially wooded Burnt Meadow summit. Here more than 180-degree views greet you, with Stone Mountain (the highest of the range's five summits) directly to the south. Around to the northwest, you may find views into New Hampshire's major peaks seasonally. A short walk west and northwest through the woods can yield views to the Presidential Range in those months when the leaves are off summit trees and brush.

From Burnt Meadow's north summit, 1.3 miles above the road, walk west next and begin the descent on the yellow-blazed Twin Brook Trail. Here you drop rather steeply in stands of pitch pine on more of the range's characteristic ledge. The route gradually pulls around to the south, and striking views emerge down the ravine between the north peak and Stone Mountain. Watch carefully as the trail changes direction periodically while it works downhill. At about 0.75 mile below the north summit, the route begins to pull around to the southeast. You reach a junction with the Stone Mountain Trail to the right shortly. (This side trail rises to Stone's open 1,624-foot summit in about three-quarters of a mile, where there are additional outlooks over the region. The side trip to Stone Mountain's crest can be added to this hike if you wish. Allow for another 1.5 miles distance and add an hour of hiking time to the totals noted at the top of the loop hike.)

Past Stone Mountain, continue south and east on the Twin Brook Trail as it drops gradually down the ravine. Keep your eye out for blazes as the trail roams down the brook's bed, often moving from side to side in the ravine. In late fall, winter, and early spring, expect to walk on a lot of fragmented ice here. In some years, snow fills in this gully to consid-

BURNT MEADOW MOUNTAIN

erable depth, and snowmelt charges the brook, draining to the east. Expect some wet spots. Tree cover has an odd look as you progress downhill, with lots of bent hardwoods evident. Near the bottom of the ravine, the trail turns more to the northeast, climbs a little, and reaches its junction with the Burnt Meadow Trail through which you passed earlier. Here you bear right and walk generally east less than a half mile, descending to the parking area and road.

Miles Notch–Great Brook Loop

DISTANCE (AROUND LOOP): 11 miles

HIKING TIME: 7 hours, 30 minutes

VERTICAL RISE: 2,150 feet

MAPS: USGS 7.5′ Speckled Mountain, ME; AMC Carter–Mahoosuc sheet

For the enthusiastic, long-distance hiker, the walk in to Miles Notch and the circuit of the major summits that lie to its west make one of the most beautiful long day trips in Maine's mountains. Located in the little-visited lands east of the Evans Notch region and north of Kezar Lake, this extended, horseshoe-shaped route provides excellent, seldom-seen views over many western Maine mountains and New Hampshire's Presidentials. These hills also have the virtue of being infrequently walked, and it's rare to meet anyone on the trail, especially if you hike midweek.

Hikers who set out on this route should be fit, experienced trail users. The first half of the route is well marked and easy to follow. Portions of the second half from Butters Mountain to the Great Brook Trail junction are brushy, not well marked, and require a good sense of direction and the ability to locate a sometimes barely discernible footpath. (Trail maintenance may have improved this section since this description was written.) You should definitely carry a map (USGS Speckled Mountain 7.5-minute series or AMC Carter-Mahoosuc sheet) and compass. Although there are brooks near the trail on the first and last thirds of the route, you should not count on finding potable water anywhere on this walk in a dry summer. Carry plenty of fluids and food with you.

You can approach the trail from either north or south on ME 5. Turn west off ME 5 in North Lovell by the Evergreen Valley sign. Follow this road toward Evergreen Valley for approximately 1.75 miles and make a sharp right onto Hut Road. Follow Hut Road as it meanders north and northwest along the lower reaches of Great Brook and past some cottages. About 3 miles from ME 5, the road arches around to your left

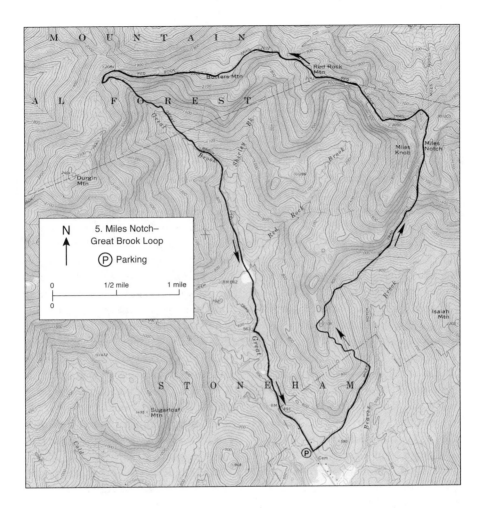

and becomes gravel surfaced. You pass several houses here and go by a cemetery to your left. A short distance farther on you'll see the Miles Notch Trail sign on your right opposite a grassy parking turnout. Leave your car here.

The Miles Notch Trail, the initial leg of this extended hike, is an attractive, wooded path that connects, on its north end, with the Haystack Notch Trail in some unspoiled backcountry in West Bethel. From the signpost at the trailhead, walk east-northeast into brushy woodlands on a grown-up tote road. Ash, beech, young maples, and red oaks lie on both sides of the trail. They are typical of the cover you will see on a large part of this walk. The area was cut over perhaps 35 years ago and has since come back in this young, deciduous cover. The beeches are numerous all over this area, and the "mast" crop that they drop from their branches at season's end accounts for this being a favorite black bear territory.

The trail rises quickly into some towering white pines and soon parallels the west bank of seasonal Beaver Brook. Little clumps of arborvitae dot the ground, and you cross a bar of granitic ledge shortly. The trail continues to follow the bed of the tote road as it works its way generally northward. Nearly a mile from the trailhead, a big log blocks the road, and mustard yellow blazes direct you left (west) along a rerouting of the old trail. Walking west and northwest here on what is not a very distinct path, you crest a small rise by a glacial erratic topped with woodferns.

Your walk continues to drift northwest in the direction of a ridge for a while. In a grove of more white pines, the trail pulls toward the east-northeast at the base of the ridge. You need to watch for blazes carefully to spot this turn. Passing some tall white birches, the trail quickly begins to lead you up some granitic ledges, still in a northeasterly direction. Views to the west toward Speckled and Durgin Mountains open up; they're best in spring and autumn. Topping the ridge among stands of oak, pass through a grove of red pine and begin a march toward the east and northeast. You'll pass a number of granite outcrops and walk through very attractive groves of red spruce and, later, aged hemlock.

The trail continues, dropping downward to the east-northeast, and rejoins the tote road at a point roughly 1.5 miles above the left turn you made earlier. Following the roadbed northward, work your way up the steepening cleft between Elizabeth Mountain (still identified as Miles Knob on some maps) and, to the east, Isaiah Mountain. The great, overhanging granitic cliffs of Elizabeth Mountain come gradually into view to your left, and you cross Beaver Brook as you again head northeast.

The walk on the final rise to the col that leads to Elizabeth Mountain can be rather steep in places and demands steady effort. Fragrant woodfern, northern maidenhair, and lady fern grow along the route. The trail climbs along the spruce- and lichen-covered side of Peter Mountain, where a sign indicates the Red Rock Trail to your left. Turn left (west) here and descend into a gully—which you go straight across—then commence a climb up the north side of Elizabeth Mountain. (From the point of leaving the Miles Notch Trail, the route west is not blazed, and at some places you may lose the path. Watch carefully.) You now climb on steady grades west and southwest through stands of beech, where there are occasional good outlooks north and northeast. The trail crests Elizabeth Mountain and begins to meander northwest through groves of spruce and balsam, where it drops into a gully and rises again. At 1.25 miles from the Miles Notch Trail, you emerge on the ledgy summit ridge of Red Rock Mountain. There are fine views both north and south along here, and the most beautiful portion of the walk lies in the next 1.5 miles. Watch for a turnout to your left where there is a good spot to picnic, with majestic outlooks over Kezar Lake to the south.

Continuing westward along the ridge, you pass many open spots with splendid views. The imposing summit to the northwest is Caribou Mountain in Evans Notch (see Hike 32), with Haystack Mountain just visible to its left. You come to a couple of points where, looking carefully westsouthwest, you can see the summit of New Hampshire's Mount Washington just visible between foreground peaks. In a few minutes you'll pass a last open ledge, with broad views to Butters Mountain and southwest to Speckled Mountain, and descend into another gully. In the low ground, cross the seasonal headwaters of Shirley Brook, then clamber up to the flat ridge of Butters Mountain. More views are available

MILES NOTCH TRAILHEAD

here over what is largely wild country. Haystack Notch is immediately below, to the north.

Once past the open summit area, the trail on Butters Mountain slabs west-southwest, staying not far below the ridge and coming back up onto the ridge from time to time. Views diminish, and the trail becomes brushy and is often blocked by fallen trees. In this section, the trail can be very hard to follow and even experienced hikers will need to use care (more recent trail work, if any, may improve this situation). The route gradually pulls around to the south toward Durgin and Speckled Mountains and arrives in a glade dense with ferns, at the Great Brook trailhead.

Bear left on this yellow-blazed trail and commence the descent on the last leg of the loop. Walk east on level ground for a short way with some layered granite slabs to your left. The ridge you walked earlier can also be seen to your left. The route soon plunges down to the southeast, losing more than 1,000 feet of altitude in the next mile. Attractive views to the valley southward open up from time to time. The trail drops steadily, staying to the north of Great Brook, and crosses both Shirley Brook and Red Rock Brook. Great Brook is just a trickle of water in high summer, but in late winter and spring, snowmelt courses down here in great torrents; the much widened, ledgy falls over which the brook passes are on your right.

About 2 miles below the trail junction at a Wilderness Area boundary post, cross Great Brook. A short distance farther down, the path pulls away from the brook and southward on a grassy tote road. The terrain flattens some and walking becomes pleasantly easy here. Stay with the yellow blazes as the tote road widens and the trail proceeds south and southeast on a network of connecting, little-used woods roads. Walk this terrain for another 0.5 mile, where you join a wider, gravel road and shortly pass over a gated wooden bridge. Continue the walk southeastward now, past several campsites and side roads. In another mile, you reach the parking area and trailhead where you began the walk.

6

Peary Mountain

DISTANCE (ROUND TRIP): 2 miles	
HIKING TIME: 2 hours	
VERTICAL RISE: 500 feet	
MAPS: USGS 7.5' Brownfield, ME	

This pretty little mountain in extreme western Maine is a sleeper. Not much hiked, and largely the province of snowmobilers in winter, Peary Mountain offers views of the Presidential Range in New Hampshire, the nearby Burnt Meadow Mountains in Maine, and other major peaks to the northeast. Hikers Ken Margolin and Judy Morrison urged me to try this quiet hill, nestled in a range of several low summits in Brownfield, and I am very glad they did. Peary offers a delightful outing in all seasons and a unique view of the major mountain groups in New Hampshire.

Standing in the varied hill country west of the Sebago–Long Lake Region and just east of the New Hampshire state line, Peary Mountain is easily reached. From the junction of ME 160 and ME 113 in East Brownfield, take 113 north 2.2 miles to Farnsworth Road, which departs west through a neighborhood of houses. (If approaching from the north, Farnsworth Road is 5 miles south of the junction of ME 113 and ME 302 in Fryeburg.) Follow Farnsworth Road, which shortly becomes gravel, for 1.2 miles to a sandy turnout on the right, or north, side of the road. As you drive in, you will have occasional views to both Frost and Peary Mountains on your left. The turnout lies just before two signs indicating "narrow bridge." Park here, being careful not to block the road.

To begin the hike, cross Farnsworth Road and enter the woods. Walk a shady tote road that runs southward on the east side of brackish Little Saco Brook, barely visible in the brush. The leafy road meanders south and southwest, rising and dipping for several hundred yards. The route crosses several shallow, dry streambeds bordered by beech scrub, young white pines, and clusters of arbor vitae. At two white paper birches,

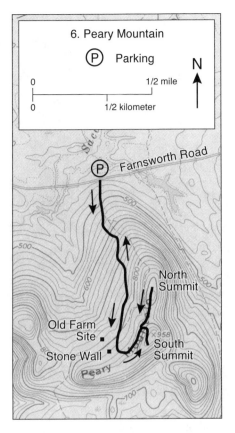

6. Peary Mountain

P Parking

N

0 ——————————— 1/2 mile

0 ——————————— 1/2 kilometer

Farnsworth Road

P

North Summit

Old Farm Site

Stone Wall

South Summit

X 958

Peary

tains. The understory is coniferous and the overstory deciduous as you near the summit ridge.

The trail breaks out into the open shortly and passes an alpine pasture to the left, continuing southwest and south. A second grassy, open area is entered where you walk another few dozen yards on a level col. Peary's multi-summit ridgeline lies off to your left. Watch carefully now for a cairn on the left, by the remnants of a stone wall. Turn left and east here, emerging in a few steps on the ledgy, rutted course of another snowmobile trail, which runs northeast. Turn left and northeast and follow the snowmobile trail as it bends eastward for a couple of hundred yards. Look carefully for a small stone cairn on the right side of the trail just before you reach a snowmobile route sign tacked to a tree. At the cairn, turn off the snowmobile trail and scramble up a steep rise to the right where a footpath is evident. At the top of this short rise the ledges of Peary's south summit are visible. Turn left and immediately right to gain access to the mountain's open summit dome.

Peary is only 958 feet above sea level at its highest point, but you would never know it. The views northwest from the broad, arching granite ledges here provide one of the finest panoramas of New Hampshire's major peaks available. The outlook is more like that from a ridge three times as high. An uninterrupted view of major peaks, from Chocorua in the distant southwest to the Moriahs in the far north, is yours for the taking. In the immediate foreground to the northwest is the drumlin-shaped hump of Tibbetts Mountain. This spot is a splendid venue to pause and enjoy lunch before moving on.

When ready to see more of Peary's ridgeline, go back to the point where

the trail climbs a little, dips again, and enters groves of hemlocks. This is dense climax forest, probably cut selectively many years ago, judging by the stands of ancient pines and hemlocks here.

The trail, a snowmobile route in winter, continues its rise to the south, staying with a shallow ravine on your left. These low spots carry runoff from above, in early spring, but go dry as summer approaches. The route next enters a long corridor of young hemlocks, which arch above, keeping sunlight at bay. The grade, rising steadily, begins to become noticeable now as the road dead ahead is suddenly closed off. You take to a shoofly diversion that goes right for a short distance until the main right-of-way is rejoined. Vegetation here is the reverse of what one expects on Northeast moun-

THE VIEW NORTHEAST OVER THE BROWNFIELD BOG TO THE LONG MASSIF OF PLEASANT MOUNTAIN

you turned just below this south summit. Straight ahead and northeast you will see another grassy, open field marked by cairns. Follow the cairns northeast and north across two more clearings on the narrow ridge, with occasional good views to the south. Views of nearby Frost Mountain lie to the southeast through the trees. Stay with the ridge path, which is occasionally marked with small cairns, and work your way to a clearing spotted by a scattering of boulders. There are excellent southerly outlooks now to the northern and subsidiary summits of massive Burnt Meadow Mountain.

Walk farther along the ridge, pulling more northward on an increasingly indistinct trail. You soon emerge on Peary's northernmost summit, a ledgy pile and field bordered by a red oak forest. At the lower end of this grassy plot you'll enjoy spectacular views of Pleasant Mountain and the expansive, marshy deadwater through which the Saco River flows. Both are seen over the north slope of Frost Mountain. Off to the north is the bare rise named Mount Tom. Other Maine summits and highlands form distinct shapes all the way to the northeast horizon. The views from this point will demand some of your unhurried time.

To return to the parking turnout, walk back along Peary's ridge to the turn beneath the south summit, and bear right and right again, ascending the steep bank to the snowmobile road and small cairn. Walk west on the snowmobile trail to the stone wall where you turned earlier. Go right on the main path at the wall and descend north to Farnsworth Road.

II.

SOUTH COAST AND CAMDEN HILLS

Bradbury Mountain Loop

DISTANCE: 3.75 miles

HIKING TIME: 2 hours, 30 minutes

VERTICAL RISE: 200 feet

MAPS: USGS 7.5′ Pownal, ME; Bradbury Mountain State Park map

Bradbury Mountain rises in State of Maine parklands of the same name in the small, rural community of Pownal, a few miles west of Freeport. This low summit supports hundreds of acres of conifers and a well-developed network of trails that lead to the mountain's 485-foot crown. Trails ascend gradually here amid densely wooded cover and provide pleasant routes for hiking in all seasons and for snowshoeing in winter. These parklands also are home to a 35-site primitive campground and, in the cold months, numerous cross-country ski trails. Bradbury Mountain's open summit ledges offer a great place to picnic and take the sun with views all the way to the Atlantic, which forms the horizon line to the distant east.

To reach the mountain, take Exit 22 west from I-295 in Freeport. Bear left and west onto Pownal Road. Follow Pownal Road (which soon becomes Elmwood Road) west about 7 miles to a crossroads at Pownal Center. Turn right and go north on ME 9 for a short distance and watch for the entrance to Bradbury Mountain State Park on the left. Enter the park (small fee) and go to the upper parking lot to the right. Park information is available at the warden's gate, and there are amenities such as a water source, primitive toilets, and a trail board by the parking area. The park's campsites lie on the other side of ME 9, opposite the main gate.

The hiker's route described here begins on the north end of the lot where you have parked. Watch for signs for the Northern Loop Trail, which begins by the trail board and follows a gravel service road northward, soon passing a feldspar mound and an old stone corral. The ledgy underlayment of Bradbury Mountain is evident on the left as you walk past in mixed growth woods. Con-

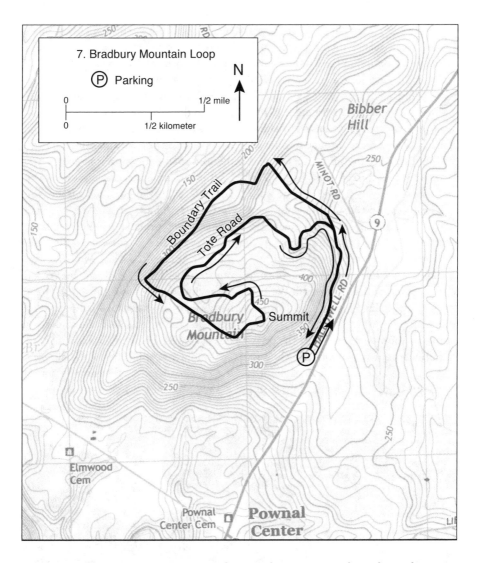

tinuing north, you pass a junction with the Ski Trail (left) and continue right and northward at a point 0.5 mile from the trailhead.

Keep right on the Boundary Trail soon (Intersection post 2) and walk northwest on a narrower path, then follow along a stone wall west over two raised ridges amid hardwoods. The stone wall marks the northern limits of the parklands, and you begin to gain some altitude here. Continue another 0.3 mile on the Boundary Trail to the park's

northwest corner where the trail turns to the southwest by a weedy tarn.

You drop southwest here for a short distance, following a stone wall through a boggy slump, and passing a connector trail to your left shortly. Climb upward now, slabbing along the steeper upland to your left as you rise to the southwest. You'll pass signage for a new trail that jumps the stone wall and runs west toward nearby Tryon Mountain. The path next ascends slowly through shaded groves of attractive, tall hemlocks, almost cathedral-like. After continuing southwest about 0.7 miles along Bradbury's west boundary, pull around to the southeast where the stone wall makes a corner.

Hike southeast as the Boundary Trail rises gently in cover dominated by white pines. Walking steadily east-southeast, you'll pass the South Ridge Trail where it departs south at Intersection post 14. The trail now pulls away from the stone wall, and rises north and northeast over grassy turf and bars of exposed ledge, emerging shortly on Bradbury's open summit.

Views from this high ledge are mainly to the east and southeast over rolling terrain, some of it still farmed. Well to the southeast lie Portland and other, intervening communities. Just visible on the far southeast horizon is the open Atlantic. In spring, a two-month-long bird count is conducted from this high perch, and large numbers of migrating accipiters, buteos, owls, and other birds are recorded as they head for northern breeding grounds. If you're hiking here during the survey period (April and May), bring your binoculars and participate in the bird-spotting event.

The return half of this hike leaves the northwest side of the summit ledges on the tote road path (signed). Go left and west dropping down through groves of hemlock, white pine, and red spruce. You descend to a small tarn, and the trail then winds southwest for 0.25 miles, crossing a footbridge. Soon, your route pulls gradually around to the north, again entering groves of hemlock. The Tote Road path widens and passes through several bends as it slowly descends northward. Some of the hemlocks here show the marks of work by pileated woodpeckers.

Roughly 0.7 miles below the summit, the Tote Road pulls to the east and passes a connector trail at Intersection post 17.

LOOKING EAST, BRADBURY MOUNTAIN

BOUNDARY TRAIL, BRADBURY MOUNTAIN

Continue east now in stands of oak, beech, and ash, passing the two points where Krista's Trail, a Nordic skiers' route, departs and reenters the tote road on the right. You walk to the northeast for a short distance, and, at Intersection post 3, turn left and north on the Northern Loop Trail. Follow this trail as it descends northwest, north, and east to Intersection post 1, which you passed earlier. Staying on the Northern Loop Trail as it widens, walk south now for 0.4 mile on the rolling ground you covered earlier on the outward leg of this hike, arriving soon at the trailhead and parking area where you began this walk. If you're an accomplished Nordic skier or snowshoer, you may also find this an attractive and challenging loop to complete in winter. A section of this trail has been relocated as it approaches the northwest corner of the park. Watch for the new trail markers.

Ovens Mouth Preserve

DISTANCE (AROUND LOOP): 3.5 miles

HIKING TIME: 2 hours, 30 minutes

VERTICAL RISE: 260 feet

MAP: USGS 7.5′ Westport, ME and USGS 7.5′ Bristol, ME; BRLT Map

One of the most attractive and varied hikes in coastal Maine is an extended loop walk through the western and eastern sections of Ovens Mouth Preserve in Boothbay. This 146-acre landmass occupies two of three wooded peninsulas that front on the tidal Ovens Mouth River. The Boothbay Region Land Trust purchased the grounds in 1994 as a part of wider efforts to maintain regional woodlands in an undeveloped state. Water views are numerous along this hike, and the unspoiled lands of the preserve give one an opportunity to witness a secluded section of Maine's riverine coast much as it was in the colonial era. Ovens Mouth is not much visited, and one can often walk here without seeing another soul.

To reach this 3.5-mile loop, drive south on ME 27 from its junction with US 1 in Edgecomb. Follow ME 27 toward Boothbay, watching for Adams Pond Road on your right about 1.25 miles north of the monument on the curve in Boothbay. If you reach the monument, you have gone too far. Reverse and watch for Adams Pond Road on your left.

On Adams Pond Road, you immediately bear right around the pond at a fork and continue through lightly settled woods and pasture for 2.2 miles to a junction. Keep left now on Dover Cross Road for a few hundred yards and turn at an Ovens Mouth Preserve sign on your right. Park in this small lot, being careful not to block the entrance. A trailboard stands here and usually contains information on these protected lands, the land trust, and local maps. Information on membership in the trust is available, too.

This hike covers both peninsulas within the preserve, beginning on the 100-acre west side. Head north on the old tote road from the parking area.

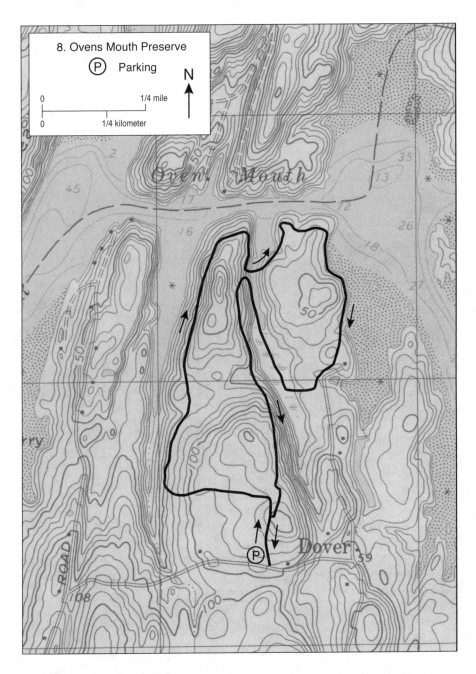

The grassy road rises gently in mixed growth, meandering northeast and then northwest. Passing through a derelict stone wall, the route arrives at a more open area, first passing a sign for the return loop of the white-blazed Shore Trail on the right. (You will emerge here at the conclusion of this double loop hike.)

Look for the outbound markers for the Shore Trail, on your left in this clearing. Turn and walk west here,

LOOKING WEST TOWARD THE OVENS MOUTH

proceeding over more or less level ground. The trail ranges into attractive groves of tall pines and some mixed hardwoods, working its way gradually north-westward. Soon you descend from the higher central rib of this peninsula. As you approach the western limits of the preserve, the trail begins to wind and descend in mixed growth, bringing you eventually closer to a salty inlet of Ovens Mouth.

Mere salt marsh at its highest point, this inlet gradually widens and deepens as you turn and follow it northward. Here the trail slabs the side of the upland from which you have just come while you walk above and parallel to the marshy inlet. Bits of exposed ledge underlie strands of varied hardwoods and young hemlock, visible from the trail as you continue northward. Some of this land was cleared in the 18th century for farming by a group led by the Hutchins, Tibbetts, Giles, and Pinkham families, who migrated here from Dover, New Hampshire. The climax forest one sees in various places is the result of clearance, regrowth, periodic cutting, and regrowth again. The route stays above the inlet for a short distance and then descends nearly to water level. Views of Ovens Mouth begin to open up here to the northwest.

At the top of the peninsula the trail scrambles eastward with good, open views of the narrow channel that is the Ovens Mouth. The tidal influx of the Sheepscot and Back Rivers enters here with a very muscular thrust. British and American wooden ships hid in the Oven farther eastward during the Revolutionary War, and local shipyards were stationed on the shores of the Oven, too. The channel ranges from 12 to 17 feet deep at mean low tide—enough to float the frigates and sloops of the Revolutionary period.

You are likely to see several Eastporters or similar boats used for lobstering moored in the current here, and mounds of stacked traps in the off season. The trail follows the Ovens Mouth at water's edge, and there are a number of ledgy spots from which to rest and watch the current. (Do not attempt to swim or wade. When Ovens Mouth is rapidly draining or filling, currents here can reach as high as 10 knots.)

The white-blazed Shore Trail skirts the tip of the peninsula, and pulls east-

MILLDAM INLET, OVENS MOUTH

ward toward Ice House Cove. This is the second inlet that drains toward the Ovens Mouth and was once dammed to maintain a freshwater pond from which ice was harvested. You will see the remains of the impoundment as you walk south above this pretty inlet. Follow the path as it slabs along the side of a hill and you come soon to the fine footbridge that crosses this cove and takes you to the easternmost peninsula of the preserve. Crossing the footbridge, you'll see what was once the ice pond to the south, now filled in by sediment and grown up in cordgrass and salt hay. The breached dam for the ice pond was constructed by William Decker and Giles Tibbetts in 1879.

Cross the bridge and turn left and north on the Yellow Trail, which makes a 1.2-mile loop around this easternmost of the three peninsulas. This trail climbs to the tip of the neck, to the right of Salt Marsh inlet, and hikers will occasionally see trail markers that are keyed to a self-guided nature walk here. The ground is sheltered by groves of very large eastern white pine, some more than 200 years old. The trail follows the easternmost part of the Ovens Mouth and then pulls to the south. Some of this ground was burnt over in the 1940s in a forest fire, but mixed vegetation has returned. You have excellent views of the Oven, a broad, shallow bay that is significantly exposed at low slack. Below it to the south is the variously named Cross or Ovens Mouth River under Burleigh Hill. Toward the center of this peninsula is the site of an early farm begun around 1790 by the Hutchins family, and bits of ancient stone walls where there was formerly pasturage. The trail follows the edge of the Oven and then pulls more southwest, in occasional gathers of bittersweet. Soon you cross a gravel road and arrive at another trailboard opposite a horse paddock.

Back under big pines, walk west and north as the loop trail heads toward the footbridge again. Along the marsh, goldenrod and sea lavender add color in late summer. The pamphlet, which describes points along the nature walk, reminds you that clumps of poison ivy grow close to the trail here, and hikers would do well to steer clear of it. Continuing north, the trail passes a small clearing and, later, clusters of distinctive red pine. Completing the eastern loop, you cross the footbridge a second time and regain the central peninsula of the preserve.

You'll get a bit more exercise on the return leg as you turn left and south now, following the white-blazed Shore Trail again. The route skirts the marsh and follows a number of switchbacks as it gradually climbs onto the central ridge you walked earlier. Watch carefully for blazes. There are stands of tangled hardwoods in this section, and you'll rise about 130 feet above the trail's low point as you continue south for 0.75 mile. Turning to the southwest, the path levels off, and you arrive at the junction with the grassy road you entered on earlier. Go left here, and walk south the short distance to the trailhead and parking area to conclude this excellent walk.

Dodge Point Circuit, Damariscotta

DISTANCE (AROUND LOOP): 2.5 miles	

HIKING TIME: 2 hours

VERTICAL RISE: 230 feet

MAPS: USGS 7.5' Bristol, ME; Maine Bureau of Public Lands Dodge Point map at trailboard

A quiet hike through majestic pines along the shore of an attractive river: That's what you'll find when you walk the 500-acre Dodge Point preserve near the pretty village of Newcastle in the heart of coastal Maine. Though not far from the town centers of both Newcastle and Damariscotta, Dodge Point is a world unto itself, beautifully forested, tranquil, and rich with varied plant and animal life. A developed network of trails runs through the preserve and offers fine walking on easy grades. In winter, snowshoeing and cross-country skiing are welcome sports here as well.

Dodge Point was acquired by the Land for Maine's Future Board from the Edward Freeman Trust in 1989. The Maine Bureau of Public Lands and the Maine Coastal Access Program spearheaded the acquisition, with funding provided by the Land for Maine's Future Program, the Damariscotta River Association, and the Maine Coastal Program. The Damariscotta River Association currently supports the management and maintenance of the preserve. The Bureau of Public Lands also encourages educational and research uses here.

Dodge Point lies on River Road, south of its intersection with US 1 in Newcastle. From the large church in Newcastle Square, head south on River Road for 3.5 miles, watching for a well-marked parking area on your left. The hike may also be approached from the south. Drive north on ME 27 (River Road) 9.5 miles from Boothbay. Leave your car here at the trailhead, where an information board will acquaint you with the trail network.

This route makes a 2.5-mile circuit of the coastal side of the reserve, following the Ravine Trail and Old Farm Road. Walk first through the gate of Old Farm

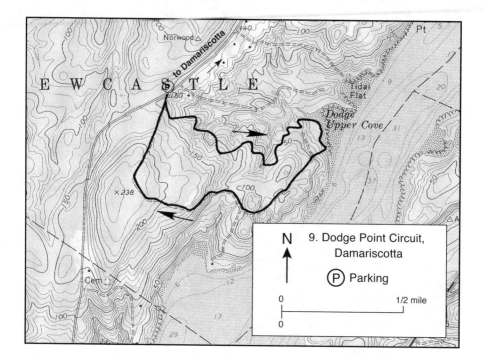

N

9. Dodge Point Circuit,
Damariscotta

Ⓟ Parking

0   1/2 mile

0

Road and continue south for a few steps, immediately bearing left (southeast) on the Ravine Trail. Walk through white pine, birch, and balsam cover. Small clumps of lycopodium, polypody fern and lady fern grow at the edges of the path. You hike up and down here over little ribs of buried rock as the route pulls around shortly to the east and northeast. You'll pass stands of red oaks and white birch. Some old pines look as if they had been ruinously explored by woodpeckers, and others have been stripped of their bark by porcupines. Certainly one of the pleasures of this walk is the interesting and constantly changing mixture of tree growth in this very attractive climax forest.

The forest canopy is higher and more open now. Christmas ferns grow under an overstory of lofty white pines. Pulling to the southeast again, the trail drops into a little spruce-filled depres-

sion and crosses a tiny, seasonal brook. Some minor twists and turns come next as the unblazed trail pulls northeast and then around to the east. Watch carefully to stay on the path. After passing some bits of sedimentary and granitic rock, the trail descends slightly and arrives at a fine old stone wall, where it turns abruptly to the south on a mossy right-of-way. The path now follows the stone wall for a short distance with big, hardrock maples on your right and stands of tall white pines on your left. Ledgy outcrops are exposed beneath the maples. Here the path is roughly 100 feet above sea level, an elevation that soon will be lost as you make your way toward the river.

After walking about 70 yards along this right-of-way, bear left into the woods and go southeast in a grove of tall pines. The trail emerges in a stand of red oaks, white oaks, and maples and runs eastward, with a deepening ravine on your left. The ravine collects runoff from its surrounding area, forms a stream, and the captured water flows northeastward to Ice Pond. Staying close to the ravine, the trail gradually pulls to the northeast and enters the fringes of a great red pine plantation that dominates much of the point. Within minutes, you turn eastward along the shore of Ice Pond. Crossing a ditch, pick up Old Farm Road, turn right, and follow it through a grove to the nearby shore of the Damariscotta River.

By a cove and stream that connect with Ice Pond, you come to Brickyard Beach. Here you'll find excellent views upriver toward Damariscotta, and downriver toward Wiley Point. Prentiss Island in South Bristol lies directly across the river. Although intervening headlands block the view, the river runs southward to the Gulf of Maine through Edgecomb, South Bristol, and Boothbay.

More than 11,000 years ago, the Damariscotta River was formed by the retreating glacial ice sheet, which gouged its streambed. Archaeological research indicates that Native Americans resided, hunted, and fished along these shores as early as 500 B.C. The river's name, "a place of many little fishes" in Abenaki, was derived from spring runs of spawning alewives farther up the river at Damariscotta Mills. A tidal river, the Damariscotta is flushed by Atlantic tides that mingle with fresh water above, in Great Salt Bay. Southward, where the river empties into the Gulf of Maine, lies Damariscove Island, site of the first (ill-fated) attempt to establish an overwintering settlement in New England. You will find old, broken bricks lying along the shore. The local clay once supported more than 20 brick foundries in this river basin.

From Brickyard Beach, walk through the grove and back up to Old Farm Road. Turn left and follow the road as it rises southward, passing the Shore Trail on your left, to a junction in a clearing. Keep right and walk to the southwest here as the road meanders through beautiful, tall stands of red pine. This plantation was begun in 1928, and further plantings continued through 1940.

You'll soon pass a firebreak on your right; continue southwest, climbing gradually. Links to the Shore Trail lead off to your left at two points along this stretch. Vegetation begins to change now. White pines, maples, and white birch characterize the next section of the route as you hike westward on steeper grades toward the highest point on this circuit. An old stone wall lies to your left. In minutes, the road broadens and passes an old shack on your right.

Many birds visit Dodge Point in-season, from the smaller species usually associated with this type of northern forest to bald eagles and osprey, which enjoy the point's proximity to good fishing grounds. As I walked along this section of the trail one recent winter day, a great flapping sound drew my attention to a bald eagle launching itself into the wind from a tree directly overhead. I wished I had been observant enough to spot it sooner, but I followed the bird's majestic flight southeastward with my binoculars. Hardly the kind of experience one soon forgets.

Leading through more red pine forest, Old Farm Road continues westward on a densely wooded plateau about 230 feet above the river's level, crossing the highest point on the hike. A stone wall

RED PINE GROVES, DODGE POINT

appears on your left, and the road pulls sharply to your right (north). The grassy track passes several woods roads, which come in from left and right. The remains of stone walls now lie attractively on both sides of the road, overgrown by vines and brush. Continuing northward through pretty, mixed-growth forest, you walk the widening road as it descends slowly, passes the Ravine Trail you entered earlier, and ends at the parking area.

Note: Hikers may also wish to add the self-guiding nature walk along the Shore Trail to their explorations. The Shore Trail departs Old Farm Road in several places. Maggie Macy-Peterson's excellent self-guide to this separate nature walk, entitled *The Discovery Trail at Dodge Point,* is for sale at the Skidompha Library on Main Street in Damariscotta, or by writing to the Damariscotta River Association, PO Box 333, Damariscotta, ME 04543. Memberships in the association are also available; call 207-563-1393 or visit them on the Web at www.draclt.org.

10

Mount Battie

DISTANCE (ROUND TRIP): 1 mile

HIKING TIME: 1 hour

VERTICAL RISE: 600 feet

MAP: USGS 7.5' Camden, ME

Later in this book, I describe some of the exceptional climbing and hiking on Mount Desert Island. Mount Desert boasts the highest peaks along the North Atlantic seaboard and views to match. But because Maine is Maine, there happens to be a second excellent area of coastal hiking near what many consider the finest yachting harbor in the East. Camden, long recognized as the place "where the mountains come down to the sea," is the center of a ring of pleasant, low mountains that provide good hiking and views nearly comparable to those of Mount Desert.

A good first hike in the area, Mount Battie offers short, steep routes to exceptional views of the Camden coastal scene. The Mount Battie South Trail rises from the northwest residential section of Camden, not far from the business district. The trail is reached by turning west onto ME 52 from its junction with US 1, just north of the town square. Take the first right, which is Megunticook Street, and follow it to a small parking space at the base of the mountain.

The trail starts behind a grand old Victorian house at the top of Megunticook Street. It's the house with the prominent widow's walk and the huge boulders in the front yard. A small parking space lies behind the house at the trailhead. Please be careful not to trespass on the grounds of the houses bordering this area and not to block the driveways.

The trail leads north from the parking area, climbing steeply up through mixed growth away from the houses. A series of S-curves are traversed, with the trail rising steadily in the direction of the summit to the north. Deciduous growth gives way to red and white

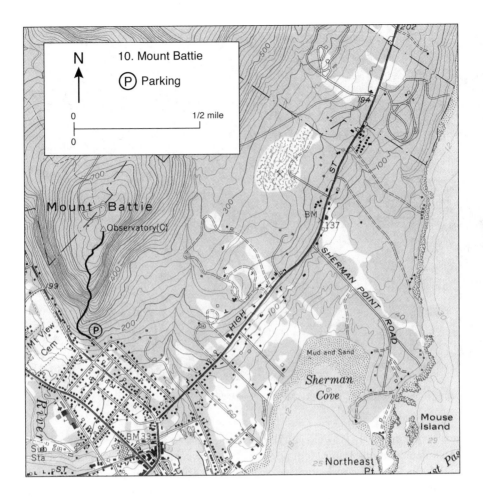

pine cover. Boulders, broken off from ledges above, are scattered about. The woods begin to thin out, and views to the south open up. Looping around a ledgy outcrop, the trail winds upward, climbing out of the trees and onto a series of ledges that will characterize the rest of the walk. Pulling first to the left over exposed ledge, the trail winds westward briefly. Crossing a plateau, the walk to the summit resumes with a quick scramble that will have you puffing. In minutes, after topping the last rise, you will walk up through low scrub to the bare summit. The whole

walk up from the road has been just over 0.5 mile, but will seem longer due to the steep rise. The views here fully compensate your effort.

The outlook from Mount Battie's sprawling summit is superb, rivaled only by Ocean Lookout (see Hike 14, Mount Megunticook). On clear days, Vinalhaven, North Haven, and Isle au Haut are visible, as are other islands along the midcoast. A stone tower marks Battie's highest point, and you'll see a bit more from its platform than you will from the many ground-level viewing spots scattered around the summit. (If you look

ON THE SUMMIT OF MOUNT BATTIE, OVERLOOKING CAMDEN HARBOR

northwest from the tower, you'll see Ocean Lookout on Mount Megunticook and the long, east-west ledgy flanks of Megunticook itself.)

Legend has it that American poet Edna St. Vincent Millay came up here often to think, and to write. The spot is assumed to be the inspiration for her lyric *Renascence*. A nice look around the summit can be had by walking around the loop made by the summit road. There are excellent views to the north as you stroll along, and perhaps find inspiration of your own. To head down, retrace your earlier route southward, descending rapidly over the ledges to your starting point. Use caution in steep sections.

11

Spruce Mountain

DISTANCE (ROUND TRIP): 1.2 miles	
HIKING TIME: 1 hour, 30 minutes	
VERTICAL RISE: 450 feet	
MAPS: Ragged Mountain Area, Georges River Land Trust map; USGS 7.5′ Camden, ME	

Some of the best news for Maine hikers in the last decade has been the advent of regional groups dedicated to land preservation and trail building. In Maine's Midcoast, the Coastal Mountains Land Trust and the Georges River Land Trust have been leaders in this activity. The latter group has stewardship over "a 50-mile network of low-impact footpaths in the Midcoast region." Establishment of new trails and protection of exceptional natural areas has helped extend hiking opportunities beyond those found in adjacent Camden Hills State Park. One of the newer coastal hikes generated by this trail-building effort is the Georges Highland Path, and its ascent to both summits of pretty Spruce Mountain. The approach to the mountain from the north described here offers hikers a short, undemanding walk up to excellent coastal and highland views amid the most southwesterly elevations of the Camden Hills range.

Spruce Mountain and its partner Mount Pleasant stand together, two symmetrical mounds, over Grassy Pond in West Rockport. To access the trailhead for this hike drive west on ME 17 from its junction with ME 90 in West Rockport. Shortly pass Mirror Lake on your right beneath Ragged Mountain (see Hike 16). Watch on the right for a parking area and trail board about 0.25 mile farther west on ME 17. Park in this lot, which serves both Ragged and Spruce Mountains.

Cross ME 17 (use caution) and look for a tree-mounted wooden sign indicating Spruce Mountain and other points on the Georges Highland Path. The trail climbs south up a rise in tall, stately white oaks. You'll soon notice a sunken stone wall on the right, the first of several such walls that crisscross

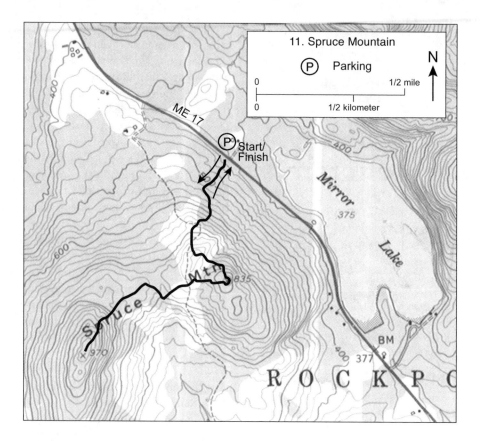

this mountain. The walls are fading evidence that these hills were used for pasturage more than a hundred years ago. In fact, Fitz Hugh Lane's famous painting of Camden Harbor and the hills that embrace it shows that nearly all of these mountains were cut over for pasturage and timber back then. Today they are reforested.

The trail meanders upward amid oak, red spruce, and birch, and soon crosses the barely visible ghost of an old tote road. Polypody ferns grow densely on both sides of the blue-blazed path, which now runs west and southwest on gentle grades. In minutes, the route pulls to the southeast and steps through a corner made by two stone walls.

Patches of ground blueberries border the path and grow in greater profusion higher on the mountain. On this shady, north side of the elevation they do not seem to fruit every year, however, as they do so reliably on other Maine mountains. In the shade here layers of deep green haircap moss flourish. Going through another stone wall, the trail pulls to the west and southwest, rising steadily.

Exposed ledge appears now as the trail continues its climb southward and enters an open spot bordered with white-paper birches. Ground juniper grows around islands of exposed ledge here. The trail narrows now, and you pass a small, blue cairn. Continuing more steeply upward, you pass a cluster of pines. You clamber up a rocky fissure now and emerge on Spruce Mountain's north summit. Use caution here if the rock is wet or icy.

This broad, open summit offers very fine views to the west and north. Stands of staghorn sumac and bayberry curl around extensive bare ledge. This summit also provides an excellent outlook across an intervening valley to the lengthy northwest-to-southeast expanse of Ragged Mountain. Below to the northwest lies pretty Grassy Pond and, beyond it, some of the low uplands trailing west from the higher range of Camden Hills. Off to the immediate west stands Mount Pleasant.

Follow the blue blazes to the sloping ledge on the southeast side of Spruce's crown and drop quickly into the woods again. Rise south and southeast in maple and oak cover next, soon stepping through a stone wall. You rise more steeply now in a grove of tall, stately oaks, unusually tall for this elevation. Bunchberry, moss, and low spruce grow close to the trail as you step onto Spruce's east summit.

Open ledge here offers views in a

THE VIEW NORTHWEST FROM SPRUCE MOUNTAIN

new direction. Well off to the east is the open Atlantic and, far distant, the southern end of Mount Desert Island. To the northeast, in the cleft between two peaks of Ragged Mountain, you'll see Ocean Lookout on Mount Megunticook (see Hike 14). Below to the east, Mirror Lake rests. Other island landmarks in Penobscot Bay are visible, too. For a mountain of its size, Spruce gives hikers an unusual number of superb, easily reached outlooks over Maine's Midcoast.

To descend, retrace your steps for 0.2 mile back to the north summit. Then, follow the trail off the dome by carefully descending northward into hardwood cover. Following the blue blazes, hike down to the north on the same route by which you ascended, reaching the roadside in half a mile. Though Spruce can be done as a short, quick hike, you'll probably want to linger on one or both of its pleasant summits and you should budget extra time for pausing and enjoying the fine summit views.

For those who want a longer walk, it's possible to continue past Spruce's east summit and follow the Georges Highland Path all the way to the Mount Pleasant Street trailhead in South Hope. If you have two cars, spot one on Mount Pleasant Street, and do an end-to-end

STARFLOWER GROWS ABUNDANTLY IN THE CAMDEN HILLS

hike from ME 17 southwest. The total distance for an end-to-end hike over Spruce Mountain and on to the Mount Pleasant Street trailhead is about 2.7 miles.

12

Cameron Mountain

DISTANCE (ROUND TRIP): 6.3 miles	
HIKING TIME: 3 hours, 30 minutes	
VERTICAL RISE: 700 feet	
MAPS: USGS 7.5′ Lincolnville, ME; Camden Hills State Park map; AMC map: Camden Hills	

Cameron Mountain rests in the second rank of Camden Hills. Not among those that line US 1 and directly front the ocean, Cameron lies back in the woods behind the first range, and orients itself more to the country toward the west. Away from the bustle of Camden Harbor, Cameron Mountain makes a pleasant elevation for taking the measure of the Camden highlands and for enjoying the bright, high breezes of a summer day out of earshot of tourist traffic. If you hike as a family, this route is good for children over six or seven, as the grades are very moderate.

This attractive jaunt into the country on the west side of Camden Hills State Park is longer than it once was. For many years, you could drive rough Ski Lodge Road right to the trailhead. Happily the road is now gated and free of vehicular traffic, and this quiet walk begins farther out on ME 173 in Lincolnville. You may wish to pick up a map of Camden Hills State Park at park headquarters just north of Camden center on US 1. There is also an Appalachian Mountain Club (AMC) map of these hills, which shows somewhat more detail than the park map. It can be found in local bookstores. Then drive 4 miles farther north on US 1 to Lincolnville and turn west onto ME 173, continuing 2.3 miles to a fork in the road. Bear left on Youngtown Road and immediately left again into the park service parking lot at the trailhead. A bulletin board with trail announcements stands here.

Go through the gate and follow the gravel Ski Lodge Road southeast, then southwest, as it rises slowly on comfortable grades. This road now is much more tranquil and pleasant to walk than when it was frequently churned to a fine mud

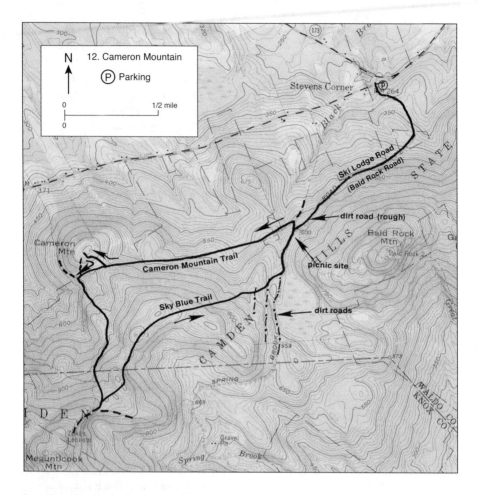

by off-road-vehicle drivers. Park rangers have performed a real service to hikers by gating this right-of-way.

The road proceeds through high, deciduous forest thick with maple, red and white oak, beech, red spruce, and ash. Great, older trees arch over the road, which continues to climb steadily. At 1.3 miles from your starting place, you reach the old Heald Picnic Area, which lies on your left under a stand of tall white pines. A trail also departs eastward here for Bald Rock Mountain (see Hike 15). Directly *opposite* this picnic grove you'll see a narrow, grassy road descending northward into the woods. Head down this road a short distance

until, on your left, you come upon Cameron Mountain Trail, which is signed.

Bear left onto this trail and follow it southwest as it rises gently between crumbling stone walls, old cellar holes, and abandoned orchards. The walk here is through very pretty climax forest, grown thick with brush on the north side and dotted with lady fern and silver glade fern. Climbing comfortably, you soon cross Black Brook on a rather rickety old plank bridge that has seen better days. The stone wall disappears and then reappears as you crest a final rise and, through a gap in the wall, see the nublike summit of Cameron Mountain in a blueberry field to your right.

You can reach the summit by a short march up an obvious cart track. (The summit is on private land, where blueberries are harvested commercially, so please leave no trace of your passing. Please don't pick the berries.) A farm pasture once occupied this place, but nature has reclaimed much of it. Other than the blueberries, the field now boasts only wildflowers such as meadowsweet, daisies, black-eyed Susans, and yarrow as its crop. Excellent views to the southwest, west, and north are yours from the summit cairn. Levenseller Mountain in Searsmont is seen to the northwest, and Gould Hill rises to the north over Coleman Pond. Bald Rock Mountain is close by to the east, and 1,200-foot Mount Megunticook (Hike 14) is the long ridge due south. Hatchet Mountain and Moody Mountain form the north-south ridge that connects with Levenseller Mountain. The pretty valleys to the west are sprinkled with small farms.

Once off the summit of Cameron, go *right* on the Cameron Mountain Trail again, and descend southwestward for a short distance. Watch carefully for a narrow, grassy road that bears sharply left (southeast). A small sign indicates Ski Lodge Road. Make the left described and walk uphill on moderate grades. This continuation of the trail will bring you up onto a connecting ridge. The deciduous growth that has characterized the route thus far begins to give

THE VIEW NORTHEAST FROM CAMERON MOUNTAIN

way to conifers, dominated by densely grown balsam and black spruce. The walking here has an attractive, alpine flavor not seen below.

Pulling next around to the south, the Cameron Mountain Trail rises higher and connects with the Sky Blue Trail at a height-of-land about a mile from where you left the blueberry field. You must look carefully for this junction. There is a lone sign on a tree to your left that's easily missed.

The Sky Blue Trail has few open views but meanders through superbly attractive country. Here you'll walk north and northwest through groves of black spruce and over a series of ledgy, open pastures. You'll pass several large granite outcrops on both left and right, and the route will pull gradually eastward, descending steadily. The right-of-way is marked occasionally with granite cairns. The path is less obvious to winter walkers and snowshoers; it's quite possible, in snow, to wander off at the trail's various turnings, resulting in some unplanned bushwhacks. A bit over a mile from the junction, a couple of tote roads enter from your right, one of which joins the trail. A short distance farther on, you emerge on the broader gravel of Ski Lodge Road and bear left.

To make the walk out to your car, proceed north and northeast on Ski Lodge Road. In 0.5 mile you'll pass the picnic area and the path opposite where you earlier gained the Cameron Mountain Trail. Continue to retrace your steps northeastward on Ski Lodge Road, and you'll reach the trailhead and parking area in another 1.5 miles.

Maiden Cliff Loop

DISTANCE (AROUND LOOP): 2.25 miles
HIKING TIME: 2 hours
VERTICAL RISE: 700 feet
MAPS: USGS 7.5′ Camden, ME; USGS 7.5′ Lincolnville, ME; AMC map: Camden Hills; Camden Hills State Park map

If sheer cliffs and picture-postcard panoramas appeal to you, the climb up Maiden Cliff, west of Camden, has something to offer both you and your camera. The cliff proves that some of the best views in the Camden hills are inland. Looming high over Megunticook Lake, Maiden Cliff—less romantically known as the Millerite Ledges—furnishes striking views to the south, west, north, and down on the extensive waters of the lake itself.

To reach the trailhead, take ME 52 west from Camden. Just before the road begins bordering the lake, 3 miles from US 1, a small, raised parking area, known as the Barrett Farm site, lies above the road on your right. Leave your car here and head north-northwest across the field into the woods. The trail follows an old logging road on a gradual rise through groves of beech and birch. The trail turns more northeastward soon, and you walk above, and parallel to, a westward-running brook.

You cross the brook shortly on a weathered log bridge and climb to your left up the bed of another seasonal brook, going northward. Pulling into hemlock woods to the right of this second brook, the trail climbs around to the northeast, rising steadily in more coniferous forest. It's cool and shady here in summer. You arrive, about 0.5 mile above the road, at a well-marked trail junction.

Go right at the junction and climb first easterly, then north as the trail ascends quickly onto the higher ground of the ridge. You are headed toward what the marker below calls a scenic trail junction with the Ridge Trail. As you ascend, there are open spots to the left of the trail with excellent views toward the southernmost Camden Hills. Pulling steeply northeast again, you emerge upon some open ledges with views eastward along Megunticook Ridge and over to Mount Battie. On a clear day, you'll see a good stretch of open ocean down toward Rockport and Rockland.

Continue a bit higher, and you'll spot a junction marker where you bear sharply left (northwest) on the Scenic Trail. Follow this path over more high, exposed ledge and through the occasional slump as it meanders over the rock toward Maiden Cliff. The views here are spectacular to the southwest and northwest, and there are a number of excellent, open places to picnic and take the sun in mild weather. The white blazes lead along the edge of the ledges and eventually curve downward to the west, where they lead to Maiden Cliff. The open cliffs are just beyond a trail junction, slightly off to your right through a grove.

A metal cross above the plunging cliffs marks the point where 11-year-old Eleanora French fell to her death in May 1864. Below you to the west lies Megunticook Lake. Bald and Ragged Mountains are to the southwest. Norton and Coleman Ponds lie to the northwest, beyond the lake. Far to the south, you can see the ocean.

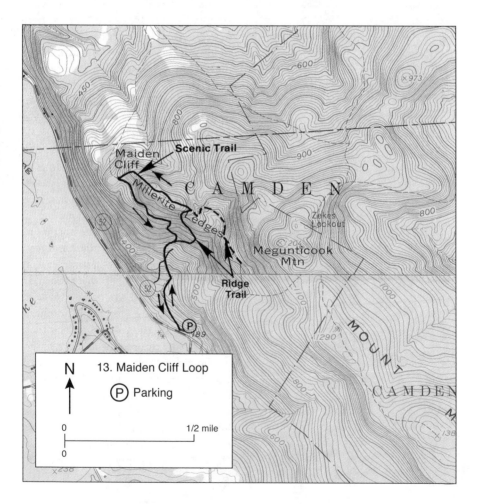

LOOKING NORTHWEST FROM MAIDEN CLIFF

To return to the road, go back to the junction of the Scenic Trail and the Maiden Cliff Trail, which you passed minutes before. Go south on the Maiden Cliff Trail, walking first over fairly level ground, then ascending a series of steps. The predominantly deciduous forest of the upper slope gives way gradually to the conifers of the lower ground as you walk back to the trail junction first passed on your way in. The junction is reached in less than 0.5 miles, and you bear right (southwest), following the bed of the brook toward your car. Retrace your steps over the footbridge and along the woods road to the parking area.

Ocean Lookout Loop, Mount Megunticook

DISTANCE (ROUND TRIP): 2.7 miles
HIKING TIME: 2 hours, 30 minutes
VERTICAL RISE: 800 feet
MAPS: USGS 7.5' Camden, ME; USGS 7.5' Lincolnville, ME; AMC Maine Mountains Trail Map—Camden Hills

Edna St. Vincent Millay referred to Camden and its hills as the place "where the mountains come down to the sea." The Camden Hills, a seaside range of low, attractive mountains, offer multiple summits with exceptional views of the Penobscot Bay islands, the entire Maine Midcoast, and surrounding highlands. The highest summit in this range is sprawling Mount Megunticook. Its Adams and Ocean Lookouts boast some of the finest broad ocean views in Maine and New England. This hike, a loop over these exceptional outlooks and others, also offers a pleasant excursion through the pretty, varied woodlands of Camden Hills State Park. For those who would like to linger, camping is available in parklands at the base of the mountain.

To hike this loop, drive north or south along US 1 to a point about midway between Camden and Lincolnville. Watch for the entrance to Camden Hills State Park on the west side of the highway. Enter the park where a modest fee for day use is charged and park maps are available. Camping reservations can also be made at the gate.

From the entrance kiosk, drive leftward up the Mount Battie Road a couple of hundred yards to the Hikers Parking Lot on the right. From the trail board here, walk a short connector trail northwest on raised boardwalks to a junction with the Nature Trail. Turn right and north here, and walk on easy grades for a third of a mile. You cross two seasonal brooks in dense hardwoods and shortly reach the Megunticook Trail. Go left now as the Megunticook Trail winds upward west and north over two courses of stone steps. The path levels some, and you continue north and northwest on widening rocky pavement on easy grades.

A half mile above the Nature Trail junction, find the Adams Lookout Trail

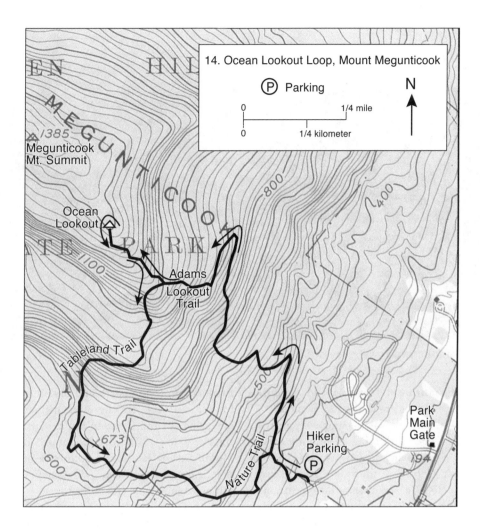

on your left. Turn here and head south, rising through woodlands grown up in spruce, beech, and carpets of wood fern. You soon arrive at the Adams Lookout site. Here you'll discover an open series of stacked ledges on the right, bordered by young oaks. Climb directly up these rock outcrops, pausing at the top to look back for superior views of Penobscot Bay and its islands. Islesboro, North Haven, and dozens of other smaller islands lie east and southeast.

From Adams Lookout, turn left and continue upward to the southwest, rising steadily in mixed-growth woodlands. In another 0.2 mile you reach a "T" with the Tablelands Trail, and bear right. The trail pulls to the west, rising more steeply over stone steps and ledge. Views open up to the south, with fine glimpses of nearby Mount Battie. Pulling to the right, you ascend farther in oak scrub, emerging on a broad, open ledge. At the top of this clearing there are more excellent, distant views to the east and northeast. On a clear day, the shape of Mount Desert Island can be seen on the eastern horizon, its highest point the summit of Cadillac Mountain. The distinctive cone of Mount Blue stands well up the coast to

THE VIEW SEAWARD FROM OCEAN LOOKOUT

the northeast. Islesboro and surrounding islands are in the foreground.

Continue west, rising over a series of ledges with more excellent views to the south and southwest. (Use caution walking here; there is a severe precipice.) To the immediate south, the summit of Mount Battie is again visible. Views open up to the west, and the long expanse of Ragged Mountain can be seen. Follow blazes over more ledge and emerge on the broad, exposed granite of Ocean Lookout. One-hundred-eighty-degree views over Penobscot Bay and the open Atlantic greet you here.

To the southeast, one can see both North Haven and Vinalhaven, separated by the Fox Island Thoroughfare. Around to the south, below Rockland, Monhegan, and Manana are visible in clear weather 12 miles out. Around to the right and west, Ragged Mountain boasts three peaks above its ski lifts.

Behind you, to the north and invisible for the moment, are the other higher elevations of the Camden Hills. With the exception of Cadillac Mountain on Mount Desert Island, no other site in northeastern America provides mountainous, blue-water views like these.

From Ocean Lookout, descend along the route you used earlier to the junction of Adams Lookout Trail and the Tablelands Trail. Pass the Adams trail and descend carefully south over some bold ledge outcrops. The trail drops quickly to a tableland below the Lookout, and you continue south over more or less level ground thickly grown up in hardwoods. The trail pulls to the west shortly and descends over a long, rock-strewn corridor and past a very large glacial erratic. The trail turns south again and drops to another tableland where it passes the Carriagelands Trail on the right in groves of hemlock, spruce, and white pine. Walk southward over sev-

Turn and follow the Nature Trail to the east, rising quickly to an expansive, open ledge bordered by white pines, ground juniper, and a cluster of pitch pines. The path steps off the ledge and runs south and east under more exposed ledge. This seems to be a side of the mountain that birds, large and small, prefer, perhaps because it's sheltered. I have heard barred owls hooting here close to the trail on several occasions. And, lower down in hardwood forest, one can often hear the brilliant, flute-like call of the wood thrush in summer.

It's through these hardwoods that you next work your way south and southeast in a series of bends, crossing two small, seasonal brooks as the grade diminishes. You gradually walk more to the northeast as the trail climbs a little and pulls rightward. You soon arrive at the junction with the short connector trail that leads to the hiker's parking area. Turn right and southeast on the connector trail, arriving in a few minutes at the trail board where you started this hike.

eral rock ribs and drop into a slump. The Tablelands trail pulls southeast and south over a ledgy mound, arriving shortly at a junction with the Nature Trail on your left.

FIDDLEHEADS GROWS ALONG MEGUNTICOOK TRAILS

Bald Rock Mountain Loop

DISTANCE (ROUND TRIP): 3.5 miles

HIKING TIME: 2 hours, 30 minutes

VERTICAL RISE: 800 feet

MAPS: USGS 7.5′ Lincolnville, ME; Camden Hills State Park map; AMC Camden Hills map

This pretty, isolated mountain is at the northern end of Camden Hills State Park in the midst of the busy midcoast region. Bald Rock does not usually experience the heavy hiker use seen in those Camden hills that lie closer to the village. The woods around this 1,100-foot mountain make for varied and pleasant walking, and there are good ocean views from the summit. Because the approach is gradual, this route can be hiked by families with children over 6 or 7 years of age without difficulty. A full canteen belongs in your pack, for there are no springs along this trail.

The path to Bald Rock no longer leaves US 1 on the east side of the mountain, but now departs from a point northwest in Lincolnville. The trail from the east side has been logged and posted in recent years. To reach the new trailhead, drive to the junction of US 1 and ME 173 in Lincolnville (4 miles north of Camden center), turning west on ME 173. Follow this road to a junction, where you keep left. Just under a mile from this junction and 2.3 miles from US 1, bear left on Youngtown Road and immediately left again into a parking area that serves a network of trails. There is a trail information notice board here, and room to leave your car.

You begin by walking through the gate onto a shaded tote road that runs southeast and southwest on easy grades. This is the old Ski Lodge Road, more recently renamed Bald Rock Road, which runs well into the forest to the site of a now demolished building. A new MFS lodge has recently been constructed. In the past, the road has sometimes been open to seasonal vehicle traffic (usually four-wheel-drive), but is now closed to motorized travel with the exception of park authority vehicles. Some parts of

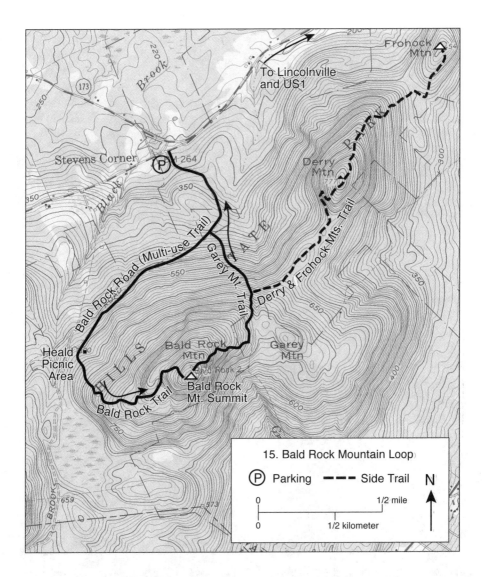

15. Bald Rock Mountain Loop

P Parking   --- Side Trail   N

0   1/2 mile

0   1/2 kilometer

this route are open to trail-bikers. The mixed hardwoods near the trailhead gradually give way to conifers as the trail rises to about 600 feet above sea level.

As the grades level out, you reach a junction approximately 1.3 miles from the parking area. Here, to your right, a trail leads to Cameron Mountain (see Hike 12). To the left, you will head into the woods on a side trail to Bald Rock.

Departing from a grove of tall conifers at what used to be the old Heald Picnic Area, the path now heads south and east as you ascend. The trail follows an old, gravelly tote road that winds gradually upward through groves of pines. The route pulls slowly through a series of bends in pleasant cover. You will cross a series of ridges and hummocks as the route climbs more steeply, gradually pulling again toward the northeast and east.

COASTAL ISLANDS FROM BALD ROCK MOUNTAIN

The trail climbs steadily as you near the top of Bald Rock, rising eventually about 500 feet above Bald Rock Road before it arrives in a grove of evergreens and reaches the 1,100-foot summit and its magnificent shelf of open ledges.

The stunning views from Bald Rock run north and south, taking in a grand sweep of the midcoast. The outlook northeast toward Islesboro and North Islesboro is particularly good. Looking due east on clear days, you may see Deer Isle farther out. Hard to the southeast, you may be able to see North Haven and Vinalhaven and, behind them, Isle au Haut, weather permitting. There are good views, too, down the coastal strip toward Camden. Many smaller islands are usually visible in the northern reaches of Penobscot Bay, and it is useful to have a chart of the bay along to help with identification. On bright summer days, there are more sailing craft than you thought existed, majestically plying these sheltered waters.

An old, rather decrepit MFS shelter is adjacent to the ledges, but a tent will serve you better if you wish to camp here. (Check with Camden Hills State Park authorities for camping permits.)

To regain the road, you can simply retrace your steps westward and down to Ski Lodge Road, and then turn right (northeast) to the parking area, a 4.2-mile round trip.

If you wish to make a loop of this hike, turn northeast off the summit in the direction of Garey Mountain. The trail descends somewhat in and out of the woods, with good views eastward for about 0.5 miles, arriving at a junction. A side trail here runs east to the 777-foot Derry Mountain, and on to Frohock Mountain, where there are more excellent views toward the islands. Opposite and to your left, the Garey Mountain Trail leads northwest off this ridge. When ready, make this left turn and walk downhill through mixed-growth cover, descending in 0.3 miles to the gravel road you were on earlier. Go *right* and northeast on Bald Rock Road, reaching the trailhead again in 0.5 mile. The distance for the complete loop walk is 3.4 miles.

Hikers may obtain a local Camden Hills State Park map that shows this hike and others in the area by stopping at the park gate on US 1, just north of Camden center.

16

Ragged Mountain

DISTANCE (ROUND TRIP): 3 miles	
HIKING TIME: 2 hours, 30 minutes	
VERTICAL RISE: 850 feet	
MAP: USGS 7.5′ Camden; Georges River Land Trust Map: Ragged Mountain section	

Ragged Mountain is a dramatic, ledgy hump that rises over beautiful Mirror Lake west of Camden and Rockport. Its brushy summit and its rocky outcrops of golden, weathered granite catch the traveler's eye from ME 17, and views of the mountain over Mirror Lake are particularly fine. Like all of the Camden Hills, this mountain rises less than 1,500 feet from the surrounding coastal plain, but its excellent summit views are those of a seemingly much higher landform. A day spent hiking here offers the same visual attractions of Maine's major peaks to the northwest and north, with the added incentive of expansive ocean views.

The trailhead lies on the north side of ME 17, about 2 miles west of the junction of ME 17 and ME 90 in West Rockport and 2 miles east of the South Hope General Store. Parking for several vehicles will be found here in a gravel lot by a trailboard.

The winding trail to Ragged descends immediately from the parking lot east-northeast into a spruce and balsam slump, goes over a seasonal brook, and crosses a stone wall and tote road all within its first 150 yards. The blue-blazed route continues north-northeast in mixed growth and then pulls north in oaks and pines with plentiful lycopodium growing along the verge.

You next cross a stone wall and then walk parallel to it, going over a knoll dotted with hardwoods. Step over another stone wall shortly and walk onto a ledge covered with patches of ground juniper. In autumn, winter, and spring, with the trees devoid of foliage, you can see the steep mass of Ragged close by to the east from this spot. Drop north across a tote road next, going over another wall in white pines and spruce amid several mossy boulders.

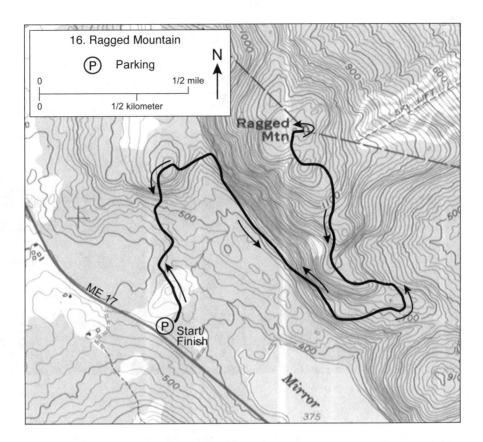

Next, follow the blazes northwest up the spine of a little ridge in beech and ash cover. You pass along a line of silver birches and more beech, crossing a faint tote road in the open. Ascend a low ridge to the northeast now in more high-canopy hardwoods as you arrive under the west slope of Ragged Mountain.

The trail has been making a long northward loop around the boggy, low ground near Mirror Lake. The route now crosses a pretty stream and turns abruptly southeast under a massive rockfall. This looming cascade of fragmented rock is testament to the work of frost in the cliffs above over many years. Standing here, you get the feeling that this isn't a place to hang around too long lest a missile from above come hurtling down. The path now heads through a

thicket of cherry, alder, and zebrawood (striped birch). Soon you step over a little braided stream and pass several large boulders in stands of tall red oak. The stream you crossed earlier has widened and now flows southward to your right.

After less than 0.5 miles of progress to the southeast, the trail begins to draw away from the stream and ascends steeply upward to the east as views of Mirror Lake open under lofty old white pines. You can see beyond the lake across the coastal strip to the open Atlantic. Continuing upward, you climb onto an oak-studded ridge in a boulder field, the granite mammoths covered in rock tripe. Here you are standing in a saddle between Ragged's main summit and a subsidiary summit to the south-

RAGGED MOUNTAIN OVER MIRROR LAKE

east. The trail next climbs quickly to the northwest, exposing dramatic, open panoramas of Spruce, Pleasant, and Meadow Mountains to the southwest.

Straddling the ridgeline, you now meander west and northwest over a series of ledges in groves of stunted oak. There are occasional spectacular views north and eastward toward Camden Harbor, Vinalhaven, and Isle au Haut here. You'll pass a number of lookouts as you make your way along the ridge. The cluttered summit of Ragged appears ahead in minutes, its terrain hosting several radio towers and relay equipment. The best views are on the southeast side of the summit near the towers.

Ragged's 1,300-foot summit offers first-class outlooks down the Maine coast for more than 35 miles. On a clear afternoon you also can see the hills of Mount Desert Island far eastward up the coast and, in dry weather, the hills of western Maine and New Hampshire on the distant western horizon. Spruce and Pleasant Mountains rise boldly above Grassy Pond to the immediate west. Other Camden hills are visible to the east, left of Camden village, the long ridge of Mount Megunticook being the most prominent. On a fair day, you'll want to remain here for a while and, I'd guess, will be reluctant to leave.

The route down the mountain retraces your steps. Use caution on the summit ledges when the rock is wet. Watch the path closely as you descend southwest and then northwest along the feeder streams north of Mirror Lake. The pleasant, 3-mile round trip to Ragged's high ground and the return to the road can be completed in two and a half hours without hurrying.

Note: This hike is part of a new network of trails in the highlands west of Camden-Rockport created by the Georges River Land Trust. This trail network represents a refreshing way to explore this countryside and deserves accolades for the new opportunities the trails provide to hikers. Maps are generally available at trailheads or from the Georges River Land Trust, 8 North Main Street, Suite 200, Rockland, ME 04841. Call 207-594-5166 or visit the Web site at www.grlt.org.

RAGGED MOUNTAIN FROM THE SOUTHWEST

Bald Mountain (Camden)

DISTANCE (ROUND TRIP): 2 miles
HIKING TIME: 1 hour, 30 minutes
VERTICAL RISE: 650 feet
MAP: USGS 7.5′ Camden, ME; AMC Camden Hills map; Camden Hills State Park map

There should be more trails like this interesting route up Bald Mountain in the beautiful Camden Hills. This path provides superb outlooks over the Camden highlands and out to the Atlantic from a breezy, open summit. The ascent is both short and undemanding with a couple of brief, steeper pitches along the way for variety. With a morning or afternoon free, you can't do better than a trip to the summit of Bald.

You'll find the Bald Mountain Trail on the Barnestown Road on Camden's west side. The road runs past the Camden Snow Bowl, and then negotiates a gap between Bald and Ragged Mountains, reaching the trailhead about a mile northwest of the ski area. A small parking lot on the east side of the road affords room to get your car off the pavement. A trail board offers current information.

The route drops quickly northeast on a boardwalk in a grove of alders and other mixed hardwoods. You walk through scattered red spruce and pine and come to an attractive stone wall on your left. In a few more yards, you cross a sweet little brook on a footbridge. Go farther northeast amid a cluster of boulders and over a broken stone wall. You then pull more to the north in a shaded depression.

The trail next slabs across an arm of Bald Mountain to the northeast. In dense ash, oak, white, and silver birch growth, you have views back over your shoulder to the looming bulk of Ragged Mountain. Climbing rapidly, go through a little hemlock stand and follow the blue-blazed path as it turns sharply southeast. Watch for outlooks over nearby highland farms to the northwest and north. The trail continues southeast through some rockfall, leveling off somewhat in ground littered with

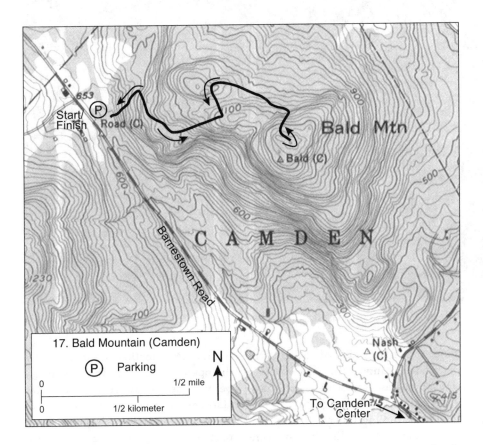

arborvitae, and haircap and sphagnum mosses.

Dropping slightly, you follow the path as it next ascends a ledgy area and then abruptly turns east and northeast. The route turns to the southeast again shortly as it moves through young stands of beech. Crossing a tiny seasonal brook, you reach a clearing on ledgy, lichen-covered granite, where there are clusters of low-bush blueberries and fine views to westward. Outlooks toward the ocean to the south also begin to open up here. The entire ridgeline of Ragged Mountain can be seen now, and you are roughly opposite Ragged's north summit.

The trail next pulls eastward on an arc with views ahead toward the summit. Opposite, the towered south peak of Ragged Mountain comes more clearly into view. Attractive Hosmer Pond lies to the southeast. Despite the steepness of the terrain, there is often a lot of deer sign hereabouts. The trail continues over a series of granite bars and runs briskly up a subsidiary ridge in scrub oaks, where you can see beyond the coastal strip to open ocean. The spindly trees also begin to yield outlooks inland to the northwest and west.

Some cairns appear. There are signs of former blueberry cultivation here, not uncommon on the high, rolling hills of Maine's coastal region. You shortly reach a grassy dome where you have superb outlooks over village steeples to the north. The trail now pulls southeast in scrub oak with the wooded crown of the mountain ahead. Within sight, the

BALD MOUNTAIN FROM THE SOUTHEAST

pine-studded cliffs of Bald Mountain's west flank plunge to the valley before you. Throughout this section you'll have excellent views to the northeast, too.

Going through taller red oaks, you pass the loop trail on the right and continue rather steeply upward in dense spruce. The path zigzags toward higher ground on what may be slippery turf. You can look back here over the dome you have just crossed. Walk southwestward around the summit dome in red spruce, ground juniper, lichens, and blueberries. Fine views of rolling countryside and inland farms in terrain dotted with ponds greet the eye here. Turning left, the trail ascends bare ledge steeply to the east and arrives on a granite slab grown up here and there with sedge and lichens. Beyond this shelf, through the opening in the evergreens, you reach another granite dome topped by a large, imposing cairn. This is the summit of Bald.

The north and northwest sides of this crown are topped with spruce, but in all other directions there are splendid open perspectives, the most direct being those eastward over Camden Harbor to the ocean and coastal islands of Vinalhaven and North Haven. Rockport Harbor lies to the southeast. You are able to see well up the coast here in the direction of Lincolnville, too. If you walk around you'll be able to spot Megunticook Ridge to the northeast. The summit of Bald is usually a breezy place, but find shelter and enjoy a rest and, perhaps, some refreshment before retracing your steps carefully to the valley.

Note: The trail you ascended is part of the Georges Highland Path and is maintained by the Georges River Land Trust. A local map may be available at the trailhead. For further information, contact The Georges River Land Trust, 8 North Main Street, Suite 200, Rockland, ME 04841. Call 207-594-5166 or visit the Web site at www.grlt.org. You may encounter some trail relocation on the upper reaches of this route.

III.
MONHEGAN

MONHEGAN ISLAND

Of all the routes open to the inveterate hiker in Maine, few are in so different and dramatic a setting as those on Monhegan Island. With its tiny sister island, Manana, Monhegan lies 10 miles southeast of Pemaquid Point and 12 miles south of Port Clyde in the open Atlantic. The island is reached by passenger boat daily (in summer, thrice daily) from Port Clyde (the *Laura B* or *Elizabeth Ann*), from Shaw's Wharf in New Harbor via Hardy Boat (twice daily in summer) and, in summer only, from Boothbay Harbor (the *Balmy Days II*).

About 1 mile wide and 1.75 miles long, Monhegan is a community of artists and fishermen, numbering fewer than 100 in winter. The island population swells in summer and, at the time of writing, four hotels and guest houses accommodate visitors during the mid-May to Columbus Day season. Camping is not allowed.

The island has an interesting history. Its fishing banks were worked by European maritime powers as early as 1500. During the 1600s, Monhegan was the site of several short-lived attempts at settlement, with control of the island contested by both the French and the British. A pirates' base of operation in the early 1700s, Monhegan may have been visited by Viking ships around the year 1100.

Present-day Monhegan will be a disappointment to anyone looking for cute boutiques and nightlife. Blissful quiet (except for a foghorn) and a sense of slowing down, reducing one's pace, are to be expected on Monhegan. Besides its cottages and few hotels, the village boasts two shops (island maps sold), a chapel, and a little schoolhouse and library. Physically, the island is shaped like a giant granite whaleback. Its cliffs plunge abruptly to the sea, especially on the Atlantic side. A hill caps Monhegan's west-central section, atop which sits Monhegan Light. The built-up area of the island and its dock rest in a hollow below and to the west of the light, opposite Manana. The village's one gravel road, with its several spurs, runs roughly north and south from the rise above the dock.

Although you can make a day trip to Monhegan in summer, you're strongly advised to stay at least overnight, and three days make an ideal visit. Be sure to have advance reservations. For more information on Monhegan Boat schedules and accommodations, call the Maine Tourism Association at 1-888-624-6345 (www.mainetourism.com) or the Monhegan Boat Line at 207-372-8848 (www.monheganboat.com).

A visit to Monhegan should take into account the very fragile ecology of the island and the reality that in high summer this island is often overcrowded with zealous day-trippers. This puts tremendous pressure on Monhegan's facilities and limited freshwater supply, to say nothing of spoiling the tranquil, remote peacefulness that is synonymous with Monhegan life. The advent of extra boat trips to the island in recent summers has increased the severity of this problem. Does this mean hiking Monhegan is out? No. I strongly urge you to make your journey in May or September and October, when the island is usually uncrowded and serene, and when accommodations are usually cheaper.

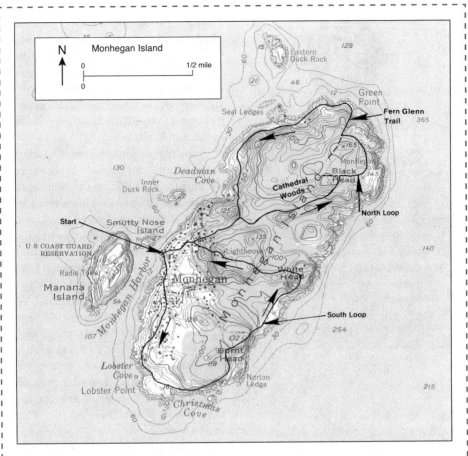

Use great caution with fire on Monhegan. Smoking is not allowed anywhere on the island outside of the immediate village area. Campfires are prohibited in all parts of the island. Trail bikes are not permitted on the island trails. Please be sure to carry away what you bring onto the island. For more information on island travel and accommodations, see the author's *Enjoying Maine's Islands* (Down East Books).

18

Monhegan
South Loop

DISTANCE (AROUND LOOP): 2 miles

HIKING TIME: 1 hour, 30 minutes

VERTICAL RISE: 50 feet

MAP: USGS 7.5′ Monhegan, ME

Nearly 20 trails link various parts of Monhegan, but there are two major loop walks on the island that include most of its spectacular scenery. The longer of these two loops makes a broad circuit of the southern end of the island and takes you by Lobster Cove, Christmas Cove, Burnt Head, and White Head.

To begin the south-island loop, start at the Monhegan Church. Walk south through the village, past the Monhegan House, and up the hill. Meandering by several houses, the gravel road continues southward, gradually running out into a grassy Jeep track. The track ends above the rocky expanse of Lobster Cove, where there are good views west toward the distant mainland. At this point, a pathway, sometimes hard to find, continues eastward through the open, thick swale. To the south lies the small ledge known as the Washerwoman, and, ahead, a similar rock rib called Norton Ledge. Watch for the rusty wreck of the Sheridan thrust up on the rocks here.

Following the edge of the land, you shortly turn northeast and north, passing Gull Rock. The trail climbs slightly, moving in and out of mixed spruce and balsam growth and over weathered ledge. The Underhill and Burnt Head Trails are passed on your left as you approach and cross Burnt Head.

Continuing along the shoreline, the route next bends to your right around Gull Cove to 160-foot White Head, one of the two highest points on the island's seaward perimeter. The views are exceptional here, and there are a number of spots to stretch out and relax on the grass.

The White Head Trail, a path which becomes a grassy tote road, leaves the head and runs nearly due west. Follow this road toward the village, and you'll soon pass a sports field on your left near the center of the island and the power station. Moments later, still walking west, you'll arrive at Monhegan Light. The lighthouse is a pretty edifice, and attached to it you'll find a small museum replete with exhibits on the island's natural and social history. Excellent views of Manana (now uninhabited) and the mainland are yours from the lighthouse lawn.

Continue westward on the now rather rocky road, which winds quickly down to a junction by the schoolhouse. Keep left here, and you'll come, in a few minutes, to your starting point on "Main Street." Although this route can easily be walked in an hour and a half, so pleasant is it on a fair day that you may want to allow several hours and pack food and water along.

MONHEGAN VILLAGE AND HARBOR

19

Monhegan North Loop

DISTANCE (AROUND LOOP): 1.75 miles

HIKING TIME: 1 hour, 30 minutes

VERTICAL RISE: 100 feet

MAP: USGS 7.5' Monhegan, ME

The loop around Monhegan's northern reaches provides an interesting hill-and-dale route through a landscape that is somewhat different from, but just as attractive as, the island's southern perimeter. This walk takes you through Monhegan's beautiful Cathedral Woods section and thence out onto the northern cliffs and rocks. Although this route can be walked in one and a half hours, the spectacular views and serene wooded areas will probably demand more of your time, and a leisurely walk of two to three hours makes a more reasonable schedule.

The Monhegan North Loop begins in front of the Monhegan Gallery, above the dock. From this point, head northeast on the gravel road past the schoolhouse. In about 0.25 mile, the Cathedral Woods Trail (Number 11) is located on your right. Enter the woods here, proceeding eastward. The trail follows the north end of a kidney-shaped marsh to your right. Momentarily, you walk through Cathedral Woods, one of the most attractive spots on the island. The woods make a quiet sanctuary of tall red spruce, balsam, and pine. The trail is carpeted with the fallen needles of these coniferous trees.

Your chances of coming across deer are excellent in this quiet, wooded part of the island. Many deer paths intersect the main trails of the island and are often mistaken for the trails. The deer paths are narrow and brush-choked, and they often end abruptly on a ledge, leaving you stranded. Stick to the marked pathways.

The trail next swings to the north as it nears Black Head and connects with the Black Head Trail (west) and the Cliff Trail (east). Turn right at this junction, following the Cliff Trail northward

A FISHING SHACK ON MONHEGAN ISLAND

through the woods and along the headlands past Black Head and above Pulpit Rock. The route soon passes a junction with the Station Hill Trail, where you keep right, continuing above the water. Swinging westward, and more inland, you reach a T, where you bear right on the Fern Glenn Trail (Number 17) and walk north to Green Point on Monhegan's north shore. This is the northernmost outcrop on the island. Turning west, it's only a short distance to Pebbly Beach. There are excellent views offshore to where Eastern Duck Island looms to the north, with Seal Ledges in the foreground.

Passing another trail on your left, proceed southwesterly along the shoreline, around Calf Cove. Nigh Duck and Smutty Nose Islands may be seen here, lying farther to the southwest on a line with Manana. There are also good views of the mainland for the leisurely walker along these bluffs.

The trail moves away from Calf Cove and Deadman's Cove, turning now to the east and south. Your route connects with the Pebbly Beach Trail, where you keep right, turning south and shortly reaching the gravel road. Walk right on the road, pass the tiny schoolhouse again, and arrive in a few minutes at your starting point in the village.

Note: Climbing around the great sea cliffs of Monhegan's eastern headlands is a tempting pastime. However, the possibility of dangerous falls into the sea is always present, and given strong currents, isolation, and undertows, rescue would be unlikely. Hikers visiting the island are urged to stick to the regular, marked trails for their own safety. Parents should use caution in monitoring the activities of children in this area.

IV.

CENTRAL REGION AND OXFORD HILLS

Round Top Mountain and Spur

DISTANCE (ROUND TRIP): 4.5 miles

HIKING TIME: 2 hours, 30 minutes

VERTICAL RISE: 640 feet

MAP: USGS 7.5' Belgrade Lakes, ME; the BRCA Trail Map to the Kennebec Highlands

More than once, a friend who lives in Maine's Belgrade Lakes region had urged me to sample the smaller peaks that ring these attractive lakes and ponds. One day I took him up on the invitation, and the ramble through these hills was a salutary one. Of the several good walks in this neighborhood, I think the hike up 1,133-foot Round Top Mountain and its connected spur is the most satisfying, and the route to its lookout views is described here. This walk is a gradual, moderate ascent up accommodating grades to a subsidiary lookout with excellent vistas and makes an ideal outing for families with youngsters.

The Belgrade Lakes region has been one of Maine's grand summer destinations for over a century. Centered on the little towns of Belgrade, Rome, Vienna, and Oakland, the area includes five major bodies of water and eight to ten smaller ponds. Long Pond and Great Pond in Belgrade, North Pond and East Pond in Rome, and Snow Pond (also called Messalonskee Lake) in Belgrade and Oakland are the larger waters at the hub of the area. Ward, Salmon, McGrath, Whittier, and Watson Ponds lie scattered over the region. There are others. The area has not been heavily developed, as many lakes regions often become. Though camps dot the shores, these villages and outlands—less than 20 miles north of Augusta, the state capital—remain wooded, rural, and quiet.

In recent years, the Belgrade Regional Conservation Alliance, spearheaded by Denny Phillips, has established a land trust in the heart of this region. Spanning several town boundaries, the Kennebec Highlands Project encompasses a number of hills and skirts many of the ponds mentioned. Traversing outright land purchases and negotiated access to land privately owned, the network of paths that

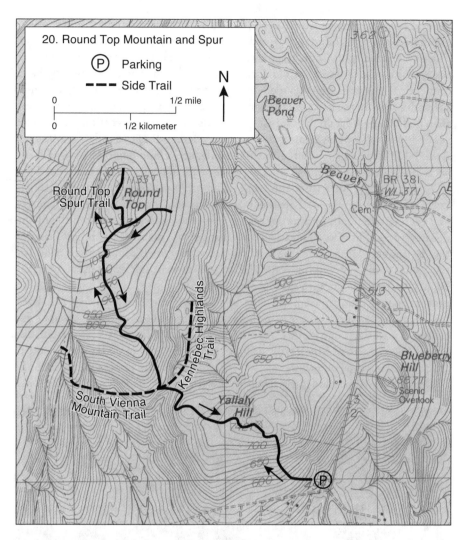

are becoming available here will make this a favorite hiking spot for persons in central Maine. The Kennebec Highlands Project is a fine example of citizens in a valued region coming together to open up new, low-impact hiking opportunities consistent with the unspoiled nature of the area. As noted elsewhere in this guide, citizen initiatives of this sort are behind a variety of new hiking possibilities in Maine.

To reach Round Top Mountain, follow ME 27 to its junction with Narrows Road 12.3 miles north of the junction of 27 and I-95 in Augusta. Narrows Road leaves ME 27 south of Belgrade Lakes center opposite a real estate office. Go west on Narrows Road for 3.1 miles to its junction with Watson Pond Road. Bear right and north here for a bit over a mile and watch for the trailhead on your left, at Wilderness Estates Road, and opposite a marker for the Dolley Trail. Turn left into a small parking area with a trail board. Please do not block entrance or egress when parking.

The trail departs first to the west and then northwestward from the parking lot and heads slowly upward through stands of spindly young hardwoods. The blue-blazed route soon steps over the granite remnants of an old farm foundation. The trail ascends a couple of hundred feet in the first 0.5 miles and then pulls to the west on the more level ground of a tableland. A limited view of Round Top's summit is visible in this section ahead to the northwest.

Approaching 1 mile from the trailhead, the route bends first northeast, and then winds north and northwest, descending slightly to a junction with the Kennebec Highlands Trail and the South Vienna Mountain Trail. The Highlands Trail, an unimproved route at present open to rough hiking, will eventually connect several summits in this hilly region west of Long Pond, allowing longer hikes, some of which will reach the smaller, remote ponds here.

Cross this low spot and the two other trails which run east-west, and continue northwest in mixed-growth woodlands as you climb more steeply toward Round Top's summit. The characteristic hardwoods of the lowlands gradually yield to conifers as a mix of species predominates at higher elevations. You reach less demanding ground in another 0.5 mile, and views begin to open up from the path to the south and to the east over Long Pond. You pull to the northeast and reach the height-of-land shortly. The trail passes a bit east of the mountain's true summit. Continuing along the ridgeline, you'll come to the Round Top Spur on your left at 1.7 miles from the road.

Leave the Round Top Trail here, bear left, and follow this short spur due northward. The best views from this mountain lie at an outlook you come to in minutes. The prospect now is to the north and east over Round Pond, French

TRAIL JUNCTION, ROUND TOP MOUNTAIN

THE VIEW NORTH, SPUR LOOKOUT, ROUND TOP MOUNTAIN

Mountain, Mount Phillip, and North and Great Ponds. You may wish to pause at this point to rest and take in these excellent megaviews of the Belgrade region. Continuing north to the end of the spur, you arrive soon at a second outlook, which provides views of Watson Pond, the northeast over Sanders Hill, and also northwest to Vienna Mountain. To visually catalogue the many ponds and lakes of the Belgrade Lakes country, there are no better viewpoints than these.

When you are ready to descend, retrace your steps off the spur to the junction with the Round Top Trail. Go right and southwest now along the summit ridge of the mountain. Watch the blue blazes as you descend southward, cross the Highlands Trail again, and then pull steadily southeastward toward the parking area.

The round trip hike over Round Top and out to its northern spur and back to the road can be completed at a com-

fortable pace in two and a half hours. Be sure to bring a full canteen with you on this hike, as there are no reliable springs on the mountain.

CHICKEN OF THE WOODS, ROUND TOP MOUNTAIN

21

Black Mountain (Sumner)

DISTANCE (ROUND TRIP): 3.25 miles

HIKING TIME: 2 hours, 30 minutes

VERTICAL RISE: 1,250 feet

MAP: USGS 7.5′ Worthley Pond, ME

Sumner is one of those nice little backwoods towns in the foothills of the western Maine mountains where the flavor of a Maine that is fast disappearing still exists. And, on a dead-end road in farm country here, you'll find Black Mountain, an inviting, low summit in the midst of the Oxford Hills. Black Mountain is sufficiently remote that you're likely to have it to yourself on most any day of the week.

To find the trail, drive along ME 219 from either east or west, and watch for its junction with a side road that runs north to Peru a couple of miles east of West Sumner. Valley Road is just under 4 miles west of the junction of ME 219 and ME 140 in East Sumner. Turn north on this side road and follow it to a crossroad where you bear left by cottages and follow another road west along the south shore of beautiful Labrador Pond. There are fine views of Black Mountain here. Passing the pond, the road turns right and north toward the mountain. At a fork, bear left by a house with a flagpole onto Black Mountain Road. This road forks in about 0.75 miles; you keep right at the fork and follow it to a point where the road ends at a "T" by a farmhouse. Park on the shoulder on the west side of the road by a yellow marker. Please be careful not to block either road. There are also several parking spaces up the west-running dirt road to the left.

There has been heavy logging in this area in recent years, and the trail may occasionally be hard to follow in its middle section. Hikers have placed small markers along the route since cutting has occurred. Additional blazes may be placed as this area gradually supports new growth. It is useful to have the latest USGS map for this area, and a compass, when navigating this hike.

Your walk begins by strolling west on the gravel logging road at this junction.

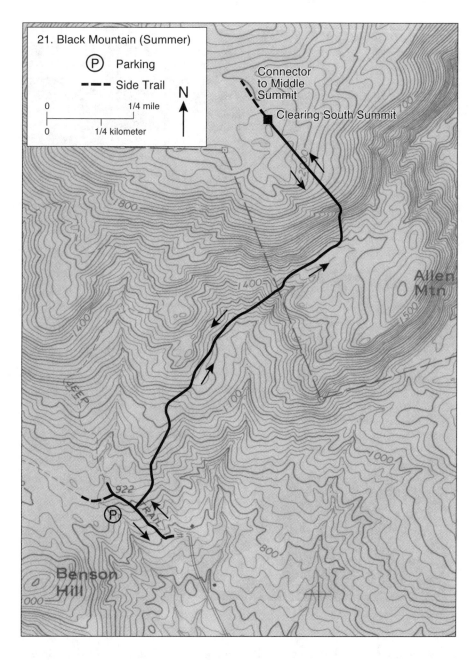

You rise quickly through grown-up former farmland laced with blackberry bushes. Stone walls border the road. In summer, this brushy terrain is alive with many bird species. Here I once saw my first scarlet tanager in years, and also Baltimore orioles. About 0.3 miles from your starting point, watch for a right turn marked by a white, arrow-shaped board on a tree. A less-used road enters the woods toward an old lumbering site here. Follow this rocky side road right and north.

The woods road, no more than a rutted track where skidders have been,

PINK LADY'S SLIPPERS

crosses a tiny, seasonal brook and pulls briefly right (north) before emerging into a clearing. The road is often damp here under the regenerating canopy. You continue north and northeast along a series of carry roads that ascend gradually. You will cross several disused skidder tracks that periodically intersect the route you are following. At these intersections there are the remnants of old timber yards, often bordered by slash.

Walking steadily upward, you turn left at a grassy fork by another tree-mounted arrow. Soon the route crosses a seasonal brook and continues upward through stands of hardwoods. Next you'll walk through another clearing at a junction of carry roads by an old stone wall bordered by piles of cuttings. The road pulls slightly left at the clearing, as you continue upward under a canopy of beech, oak, and ash. In still another clearing you pass what may have been an old foundation on the right, now reduced to a mere rock pile. Continue straight through a diagonal intersection with a carry road that plunges downward and off to the left.

The road rises further and soon becomes more grassy and indistinct, the path cleaving to its left side. You rise to a flat spot now and bear sharply right as the carry road turns more to the northeast and east. Broad views back to the southwest begin to open up. Black's lower slopes are dotted with Canadian goldenrod, Clintonia lilies, blackberries, sarsaparilla, meadow rue, self-heal, cinquefoil, bluets, wild oats, clover, and violets. Passing a stone wall, you can occasionally see the summit ridge over the tops of trees. At 0.75 miles, the route levels off and pulls around to your right (east). You soon cross a brook bed

HIKERS TAKE IN THE VIEWS ON BLACK MOUNTAIN'S LEDGY SOUTH SUMMIT

by some white paper birches, and then resume your ascent.

The trail, now narrower and rocky in places, heads more directly toward Black's easternmost 2,080-foot summit. More views open up in the direction of Evans Notch. Cross a tote road grown high in wheat grass, as you skirt the nearby nub of Allen Mountain, and you follow a still narrower trail more to the left and north for a short distance. You come shortly to the junction of two major carry roads that run through a large cut. By any stretch of the imagination, you're in moose country, and you may see tracks in soft ground. There are liberal scatterings of blowdown and slash in this section of the hike.

The trail climbs the right side of this open cut and reenters the woods in low stands of coniferous growth. You climb more steeply up a mossy cataract amid red spruce and balsam. Some low cairns indicate where the trail turns suddenly to the right and then up a low track marked by exposed ledge. Patches of haircap and sphagnum moss border the trail under spruce cover and along past pockets of blowdown. Going east-northeast, the path slabs the side of the summit dome and crosses several seasonal brooks and seeps. The trail, increasingly obscure, crosses more granite ledge carpeted with lichen, and passes some trees marked with ribbons at the top of the cut. The trail pulls to the north and northwest briefly and then northeastward amid spindly spruce, shortly arriving on the summit ledges.

The summit is open and rangy, bordered by evergreens. A walk around its perimeter will reward you with distant views of Tumbledown Dick, Brown, Thompson, and Ragged Jack Mountains to the northeast and east. Bear Pond lies to the southeast and Lake Anasaguticook to the east. A short trail leads northwest from the summit ledges to the mountain's slightly higher middle summit, once served by another trail. Carry a compass and map if you attempt to reach the other summit.

To descend, retrace your steps, staying with the main route at the many crossings on the west side of the mountain. Since there are no reliable springs on this trail, it's wise to carry plenty of drinking water, whatever the season. Given the cutting and regrowth on the lower parts of the mountain, it is wise to study the map that accompanies this hike and the larger USGS map carefully before setting out, so that, despite logging, you have a good sense of the terrain.

Mount Pisgah Loop

DISTANCE (AROUND LOOP): 2.1 miles

HIKING TIME: 2 hours

VERTICAL RISE: 450 feet

MAP: USGS 7.5′ Wayne, ME

Mount Pisgah returns to this guide-book in recognition of expanded hiking opportunities and general trail improvements. The old warden's path to the summit has long disappeared in the underbrush. Now a fine hiker's loop created in its place offers a pretty walk on both sides of the rise, and outstanding views over two states from its old fire tower. The mountain terrain over which the trail circles is now protected through the efforts of the Kennebec Land Trust and the town of Winthrop, Maine.

More than 140 years ago, much of this elevation was the site of extensive progressive agriculture by a well-respected local farmer, Dr. Ezekiel Holmes, a major supporter of the former Maine College of Agriculture at Orono. Large areas of the mountain were cleared for pasturage and cultivation at what was known as Mount Airy Farm. Maple sap was harvested from the many hard rock maples on the mountain's lower slopes. The hill farm has disappeared, and today the mountain has gone back to attractive woods. Still, here and there, one sees remnants of the ancient farm. Lone fruit trees stand marooned in what has become mixed growth forest, and many stone walls that kept in the farm's Jersey herd even now intersect today's trails.

To reach Pisgah, travel ME 133 west from Winthrop or east from Wayne. Watch for an intersection with Fairbanks Road, which departs southward from 133 just west of Berry Pond. Follow this street to where it meets Mount Pisgah Road and turn left. Continue south on this road as it passes farm fields, crosses a bridge at the connector between Wilson and Dexter Ponds, and rises to the trailhead on the left less than a mile farther south. There's adequate parking in the lot here or along the roadside opposite. The former towerman's cabin once stood beside this parking area, but it has been long since removed, as were so many others like it, when the State of Maine ceased manning its fire towers in 1991.

Begin this hike by walking up the gated gravel road barely 30 yards and turning northeast (left) into the woods by a trail register and sign. Here you walk along the new Tower Trail, winding north and northeast through groves of hardwoods in low, moist ground bridged by stone steps. The land here has been captured mostly by hardwoods, among them some of the remaining big maples that were tapped for syrup-making so many generations ago. Scattered gla-

cial erratics and occasional blowdown lie about, mixed with older stands of white pine and a variety of hardwoods. The trail widens and rises to the northeast and north on easy grades, passing shortly through a stone wall and along a raised log walkway. The walking may be muddy here in the spring, thus more stone steps and log walks are found. You'll see another of the mountain's many old stone walls alongside the path to your right, which you soon cross. Sometimes one sees here an ancient pear or apple tree, now near-buried in new growth, its branches barren.

Next the path turns to the east and southeast for a short distance, goes past an oddly bent old maple, over stone

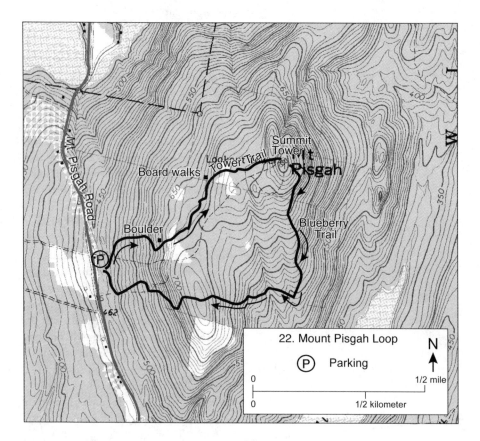

22. Mount Pisgah Loop

Ⓟ Parking

N

0   1/2 mile

0   1/2 kilometer

stairs, and around a fractured trailside boulder. You pull to the northeast again, climbing steadily in stands of old white pines. Several species of hawks patrol this mountain, and I have seen red-tails along here. Strings of lycopodium and patches of bunchberry provide ground cover. The preponderant beech and ash hardwoods below now give way to white pines and hemlocks as the trail levels off and follows another series of log walks. The trail runs through a wet section also bridged by stone steps, working its way more toward the east-northeast within this grove of conifers. Passing downed pines, you go by what appears to have been a primitive well hole on the right and shortly note a faint path coming in on both left and right. Continue straight ahead, following the blue blazes to the east under more pines as the path narrows and approaches the summit clearing. Here you pass a large, stone cairn, drop through a slump, and then follow the path over ledge and rightward up some steps to the open summit field. To your left is more ledge now and, above it, the old Maine Forest Service fire tower, erected in 1949.

The tower has had some maintenance in recent years, but still should be climbed with caution, especially with youngsters. From its cabin, the tower offers truly outstanding 360-degree views. On a clear day, one can see the oceanside Camden Hills on the horizon far to the east, and New Hampshire's Mount Washington, northern Presidential Range, and Carter-Moriah Range away to the west. Maine's higher mountains, including Mount Blue, Old Speck, Baldpate, and Saddleback lie far to the northwest. Well off to the westsouthwest is the long loaf-of-bread shape of Burnt Meadow Mountain in Brownfield. To the west lies Androscoggin Lake in the middle distance. It's not uncommon here to see hawks and turkey vultures soaring on the muscular wind currents that often sweep over the summit.

When you're ready to move on, cross the relay tower service road and reenter the woods to the southeast and south (the trailhead is now marked with a small sign; look for a board attached to a tree). The blue-blazed Blueberry Trail drops slowly southward in mixed growth woods marked by stands of blasted old pine and hemlock. The land drops off to the east on your left, and you step through a stone wall. This side of the mountain was once also involved in agriculture more than a century ago. Here and there you'll catch glimpses off to the east in the colder months when the trees are bare. The path meanders generally southward at about the 600-foot contour line, passing through more pretty, mixed-growth forest and stone walls. Soon you descend to two seasonal brooks in oak and beech cover.

You'll cross the first brook on a footbridge, and then the trail begins to climb again as you turn west and northwest over a series of split-log walkways. Soon you cross the obscured remains of a long-abandoned tote road and step over a second brook. In minutes the path quickly dips to a third seasonal brook where a sign marks the halfway point on the Blueberry Trail. The path now rises more noticeably to the northwest and west. It passes through another stone wall as it climbs back up to the height of the ridge in mixedgrowth forest dominated by white pines and bright patches of polypody fern. You walk steadily upward, leveling off in a pine grove. On the return, you have

MOUNT PISGAH TOWER VIEW

walked nearly the whole length of the mountain, and the trail will now turn and notch its way back to the northwest and the road.

Cross another abandoned tote road, and begin the descent to the west along a white-pine-shaded stone wall. The trail drops steadily west and southwest following remnants of another woods road. It then pulls northwest where you will see a cairn and several large stone erratics deposited here by glaciation.

You pass along more stone walls now as the trail turns to the north on more level ground in stands of old, expired white pine.

The descent resumes as you turn southwestward shortly on a pronounced drop in a grove of hemlocks. Go over a log walkway, and then walk again to the northwest as you progress alongside another obscure tote road to the right. The trail continues to the northwest and goes through a

tumbled stone wall. The grade slackens now and the ground levels off. Walk a few dozen more yards and you soon emerge onto the gravel road by the gate you passed when beginning this hike. Turn left and continue a few steps downhill to the parking lot where you began earlier.

23

Bald Mountain (Woodstock) and Speckled Mountain (West Peru)

DISTANCE (ROUND TRIP): 4 miles	
HIKING TIME: 3 hours	
VERTICAL RISE: 1,500 feet	
MAP: USGS 7.5′ Mount Zircon, ME	

For the boastful hiker who'd like to claim two distinct summits in a single outing, this walk will do nicely. The route described here takes in the summits of two beautiful, pillarlike mountains that rise in the midst of three remote ponds in west-central Maine. That this outing lies in backcountry, far from the madding highway, makes for just that much more hiking enjoyment. A relatively short hike (4 miles), this circuit nonetheless involves some steep sections that provide the feeling of the bigger hills to the north, and the superb, panoramic views simply enhance this impression.

Bald and Speckled Mountains can be reached by traveling ME 219 east or west to the town of East Sumner and turning north on Valley Road 3.3 miles west of the elementary school. Follow this side road for about 1.5 miles, then head left (west) on Labrador Pond Road—which runs along the south end of this pretty body of water, with its fine views of nearby mountains. You shortly join another road that comes in on your left, and continue north, bearing left on Black Mountain Road at an old schoolhouse now converted into a dwelling. Leave Black Mountain Road just under 2.5 miles from the schoolhouse to go left on Redding Road. From this junction, drive 4.9 miles to Shagg Pond. At the tiny public landing, you'll have excellent views across the pond of both of the mountains you'll hike. Drive 0.5 mile beyond Shagg Pond and up the hill on an increasingly rough road. Near the top of the incline, you'll find on your left a gravel space big enough for several cars. Park here opposite a sign reading FIRE LANE 1010.

Begin your walk by heading southeast and east on the gravel fire lane under a tall canopy of beeches. The ter-

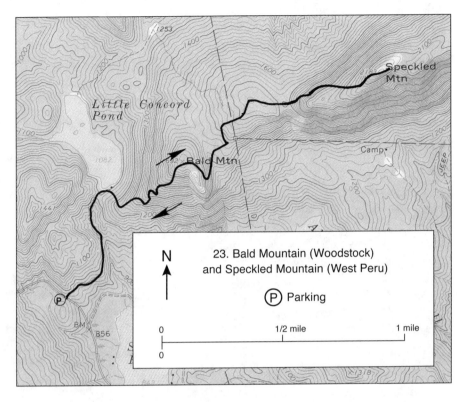

N

23. Bald Mountain (Woodstock) and Speckled Mountain (West Peru)

(P) Parking

0   1/2 mile   1 mile

0

rain here is attractive, particularly in autumn when through the trees there are glimpses of Shagg Pond. Dropping gradually to the east, the road pulls around to the north over a seasonal brook and through a grove of hemlocks before crossing a rib of exposed ledge. Passing a rocky overhang on your right, the route drops farther into a slump and divides into three tracks, any one of which will take you over the next rise, where the tracks merge into one again. The path now continues along the wide fire lane to the northeast and north, arriving after about 0.6 mile at Little Concord Pond.

Just before you reach the shore of this attractive pond, bear right on a blue-blazed trail and climb directly up a ledge to your right. Under hemlock and red spruce, the route climbs briskly east and southeast on exposed ledge sprinkled with mica schist and quartz-ite. Views to the west and south soon begin to open up. The trail meanders eastward while rising steadily, passes a downed birch, and plateaus briefly, offering more views over Shagg Pond and the hills to the west. Tall white pines and hemlocks provide cover over this narrow, eastward-trending rib of land as you walk upward. Some old pines in this section have been reduced to ruins by pileated woodpeckers searching for insects in their trunks.

The trail next moves through a stand of red oak and birch, where views to the north open up occasionally. Meandering still upward toward the east, the trail soon crests on the summit ledges of Bald. There must be an acre of open ledge here, with spectacular views to the ranges immediately west and southwest. Shagg Pond provides a mirrorlike surface

SPECKLED MOUNTAIN FROM THE SUMMIT OF BALD MOUNTAIN

far below. On a sunny day, it's so pleasant here that you'll just want to sit, eat lunch, and enjoy the grand perspective ranging from southeast to northwest.

When you're ready to take in your second peak of the day, follow the ledges through clumps of rhodora to the southeast and east, watching for blue blazes. You'll enjoy an excellent view of Speckled Mountain here just before you reenter hemlock and spruce woods and descend steeply to the northeast. Drop into stands of beech on a boulder-strewn col between the two mountains where fine views southward toward pretty Abbott Pond occur. Crossing a seasonal brook and a snowmobile trail, continue east-northeast on level ground and enter spruce woods again on the blue-blazed trail, shortly passing a low stone plinth marked "1916."

Now continue north-northeastward through alternating open, ledgy clearings and shady corridors of spruce. Cairns or boulders mark the clearings. Clumps of chalk green lichen, borders of haircap moss, and low-bush blueberries line the shaded trail. You soon pull east in a corridor of black birch at the top of the col and walk directly east to the steep west face of Speckled Mountain. Here your work begins again.

The trail now heads right up Speckled, where good outlooks to the northwest can be seen. The grades are continuously steep for a short distance, and then the route moves under the west ledges of Speckled, turns south, and climbs quickly onto those ledges. Dikes of quartzite and deposits of mica schist and feldspar glint in the granitic rock. Magnificent views to the northwest and west are yours here. The tree-studded ridge of Bald Mountain lies immediately back to the west.

The route now slabs along the north side of the ridge, rising steadily through low spruce and passing through a series of open ledges with domelike formations. Broad outlooks to the south open up through the trees. In a few more minutes, you emerge on the summit ledges marked by an old US Geodetic Survey seal and the figures "2207" carved in the rock.

The scene here deserves the term "spectacular," with views in nearly all directions. There are, in fact, too many mountains visible from here to be listed easily. On a bright day, you can count perhaps 40 summits of varying elevation around the horizon, giving you the feeling that Speckled is more lofty than its modest 2,200 feet would suggest.

When you're reluctantly prepared to leave this attractive summit, retrace your steps west to Bald Mountain, watching for the familiar blue blazes all the way to Little Concord Pond and thence out the fire road to where you parked.

The trail described here is currently well maintained by Roger and Laurie Doran.

24

Rumford Whitecap

DISTANCE (ROUND TRIP): 5 miles

HIKING TIME: 3 hours, 30 minutes

VERTICAL RISE: 1,625 feet

MAP: USGS 7.5' East Andover, ME

Rumford Whitecap stands like a great stone loaf over the valleys of the Androscoggin and Ellis Rivers. The mountain ranges west to east, a lengthy pluton of bright granite and schists, bordered on its lower flanks by dense, mixed-growth forest. The old route up the mountain from the north, where there had been periodic logging, is no longer in use, and a newer trail now ascends from the southwest. Summit lands and most of the route are now protected through the work of the Mahoosuc Land Trust. The mountain offers a pleasant, invigorating climb to a broad, open summit ridge with splendid views. The route to the summit is gradual and slabs the side of the mountain generally to the northeast, rising to many acres of bare ledge and scrub.

Approach Rumford Whitecap from east or west on US 2 and, just west of Rumford Point, turn north on ME 5 toward Andover. Follow ME 5 for 3 miles and turn right, crossing the Ellis River, and then keep left and north on East Andover Road. Follow this road north a short distance and turn into a parking area by a trail board on your left. (The old trailhead on Coburn Brook Road is no longer in use.)

To begin this hike, cross East Andover Road and follow a gravel road through a clearing. You shortly pass through a gate and, beyond it, proceed north-northeast on an old tote road, the route indicated by orange blazes. Continue northeast through pretty mixed-growth woods of beech, ash, red spruce, hemlock, and balsam. Several side roads or skidder trails depart the route in this section. Stay on the main trail as the grade increases. The road narrows some and leans northward. Next, you pass a connector trail that

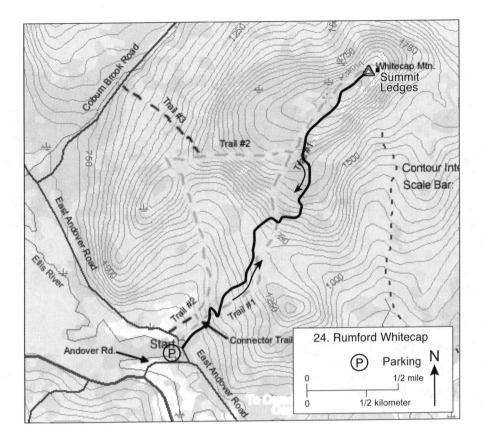

runs to the left and continue upward in a section where several seasonal brooks cross the trail.

The route abruptly pulls to the south and southeast for a short distance and then runs upward again to the northeast, going through a clearing. Continue northeast, avoiding several tote roads that lead left and rise along a grassy path that becomes a mere double-track shortly. Watch for a small cairn here that indicates the route. Walk eastward and then southeast, after which the trail turns to the northeast again and begins to enter the terrain that characterizes the upper slopes of the whitecap.

Hikers will see more of the stone underlayment now and often topsoil gives way to walking directly on granite as you proceed. These exposed granite lanes often become channels for run-off during rainy weather and may get your boots wet. Broad sheets of moving water slide downhill beneath the mossy cover. There is evidence here, as on so many Maine uplands, of how thin the topsoil can be and how fragile is its hold on the mountain. In this area you will pass, on your left, a signed trail that is a remnant of the old approach from the west. As you ascend now, deciduous cover gradually yields to stands of conifers. Ground cover includes a variety of mosses, lycopodium, bearberry, and sedge.

The foliage soon begins to thin, and you can peer ahead toward more open terrain in the direction of the

LOOKING SOUTHWEST FROM RUMFORD WHITECAP'S OPEN LEDGES

summit. You cross a small seasonal brook and then follow it briefly as you climb on steeper grades. Fine views of mountains to the west and southwest emerge as the trail meanders north and east and climbs steadily. Tree cover becomes progressively sparser, and the terrain is littered with glacial erratics, both large and small. A final rise leads you shortly to the summit ledge, totally in the open on a sea of brilliant rock.

As they say, It's a different world up here. The summit ledge provides outlooks in all directions. To the immediate east lies the mill city of Rumford and the long cleft of the Androscoggin River valley, with antenna-topped Black Mountain in the foreground. To the north-northeast, on a subsid-iary ridge, are an unexpected line of tall wind generators, creating power for Maine and the New England grid. Back to the northwest and north you'll see a perfect bowl-like cirque backed by a range of mountains. A worldwide communications satellite antenna has been situated here, the terrain perfectly suited to enhanced transmission and reception.

In the distance to the west and southwest are mountains around Evans Notch and, in New Hampshire, peaks in the Carter-Moriah Range and the Presidential Range. On clear days, Mount Washington, New England's highest summit, may be visible. Off to the far northeast lie ledgy Tumbledown Mountain and the distinctive cone of prominent Mount

Blue. So many elevations are seen here that it's no exaggeration to say that you are in the midst of a tangle of mountains on Whitecap's summit.

Rumford Whitecap collects wind the way kids collect candy, so come prepared for it when you climb here. Extra clothing, raingear, food, and water belong in your pack, especially in the shoulder seasons. Because there are parts of this route not heavily blazed, carrying this hike's map and a compass with you is essential.

To make the descent, retrace your steps southwestward, being careful not to drift onto several side-paths and openings. You will pass an alternate route where you spotted a sign on the way up. That route follows a couple of sections of the old path and then travels the connector you went by earlier. Descending on this alternative path isn't recommended or described here as it contains exposed sections that may be difficult for some hikers, especially when wet or icy. Stay with the trail you came up on and have a pleasant walk out to the trailhead.

HIKERS DESCEND SOUTHWESTWARD NEAR RUMFORD WHITECAP'S HIGH POINT

Mount Will Loop

DISTANCE (ROUND TRIP): 3.3 miles	
HIKING TIME: 2 hours, 30 minutes	
VERTICAL RISE: 1,100 feet	
MAP: USGS 7.5′ Bethel, ME	

Mount Will is a component of a long north-south upland marked by steep ledges along its southeast side, with excellent views over the upper Androscoggin Valley and to major hills to its north. The 1,726-foot mountain's south cliffs offer a first-class outlook toward Mount Abram and dozens of low mountains in Oxford County. This route carries hikers through mixed terrain and meanders over northern summit ledges, through dense hemlock forests, and to sheer promontories. The mountain lies in both Bethel and Newry, and the Bethel Conservation Commission has developed the trails described.

The triangular loop you will walk here runs through parts of the 115-acre Bethel Town Forest, but most of the route lies in private holdings. To ensure continued access to these mainly privately owned highlands, hikers should leave no trace of their passing. The Mount Will circuit seems just the right length for a solid day-hike with time out for lunch atop the ledges of the mountain's South Cliffs. It's a challenging hike, perhaps more so than its moderate height and length would suggest.

Reach the trailhead by traveling east from Bethel or west from Newry on US 2. The trailhead and raised parking area are on the north side of US 2, opposite the Bethel transfer station. The trail departs the parking area to the west and north in young hardwoods, and rises quickly to a trail junction where you keep right on the blue-green blazed North Ledges section of the loop. On this first leg of the trail you will rise over 600 feet in mixed-growth cover. You climb steadily northwest, passing around and over occasional rock ribs, which may be slippery in wet or colder weather. As you ascend, the trail climbs more steeply,

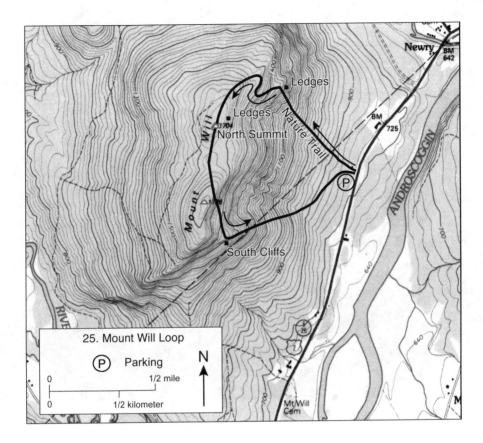

25. Mount Will Loop

P Parking

N

0 — 1/2 mile

0 — 1/2 kilometer

and periodic views open up through the scrub to your right or northeast. The trail soon notches leftward and southwest for a short distance and then rises steadily again to the northeast. You next turn west and southwest at the top of the rise, where you'll find further views, especially to the east.

Forestation at this altitude is mainly coniferous now as you walk the second section of the trail at a height of about 1,350 feet. The trail progresses southwest over several exposed patches of stone known as the North Ledges and, at 0.75 mile above the road, rises to a small opening. Pause here for views northward to rangy 3,133-foot Puzzle Mountain and to adjacent Plumbago Mountain. Far to the northeast you may

be able to see Rumford Whitecap (see Hike 24).

You continue southwest and south now along the ridgeline and soon reach the highest points on the mountain at roughly 1,725 feet. Continue south in dense cover. You are walking along the upper edge of the high ground here. Old stands of hemlock shade the path, which skirts the edge of the upland where it drops off sharply to the east. Periodically you'll find small openings in the tree cover where low-bush blueberries flourish in high summer. The path rapidly drops some 350 feet in about a half mile, descending quite steeply between several level stretches. Watch your footing carefully.

About 1.2 miles from the North

VIEW SOUTHEAST FROM MOUNT WILL'S SOUTHERN CLIFFS

Ledges you crossed earlier, you reach the South Cliffs where there are broad 180-degree views of the Androscoggin River Valley. Here atop the ledges, hikers will find several points to rest and survey the terrain opposite. It's a great picnic spot. The village of Bethel appears to the south, and Swan Hill and Farwell Mountain lie across the Androscoggin to the southeast. Stretches of cultivated land spread beyond the river. One-thousand-nine-hundred-foot Mount Abram in Locke Mills is also on the distant horizon to the southeast.

Having already descended considerably from Mount Will's highest point, you now turn northeastward on the final leg of this triangular route. It's all down hill from here, but be prepared for further steep footwork. In the next mile, you'll hike east and northeast on pronounced grades to the valley floor. The

MOUNT WILL, SOUTHERN CLIFFS OVERLOOK

route descends through mixed-growth woodlands and loses about 730 feet of elevation in that mile, most of it in the half mile immediately below the South Cliffs. This grade levels off occasionally, but the trend is to continue quickly downward. The slope becomes more gentle just above the 800-foot contour line as you proceed east to the trail junction you walked through on the ascent. In stands of younger hardwoods, bear right and south at the junction, and continue the short distance to the trailhead, completing the 3.3 mile circuit.

V.

EVANS NOTCH REGION

Deer Hill Loop

DISTANCE (ROUND TRIP): 4 miles

HIKING TIME: 2 hours, 30 minutes

VERTICAL RISE: 1,000 feet

MAPS: USGS 7.5' Center Lovell, ME; USGS 15' North Conway, NH; Chatham Trails Association Map of CTA Service Area; AMC Evans Notch map

Deer Hill, with its two east- and west-leaning summits, rises 1,367 feet above the Cold River intervale south of Evans Notch. Little Deer and Big Deer, as the summits are often called, provide hikers with splendid views of the intervale itself, the high peaks to the west and the several summits to the east served by the Conant Trail (see Hike 27). The two Deer Hills, though of modest size, provide those who make the four-mile circuit over its two high points a good half-day workout in pretty country off the beaten path. The views are so rewarding you'll want to linger.

From north or south, travel ME 113 to the trailhead near the AMC Cold River Camp in North Chatham, NH. (If approaching from the north, take ME 113 where it departs US 2 southward in Gilead. From the south, join ME 113 from the village center in Fryeburg and drive

LOOKING ACROSS TO THE BALDFACES FROM LITTLE DEER HILL

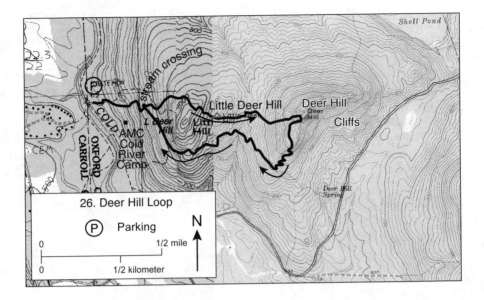

26. Deer Hill Loop

Ⓟ Parking   N

0   1/2 mile

0   1/2 kilometer

northward. ME 113 wanders across the New Hampshire state line for a couple of miles and then back into Maine as it climbs to Evans Notch.) Drive to the Baldface Circle parking area on the east side of ME 113 just north of the AMC Cold River Camp entrance.

From this point, walk the Deer Hill Connector trail as it runs eastward for a short distance. The trail drops to Charles Brook, skirts Cold River Camp, and continues to a dam on an attractive stretch of the Cold River at 0.4 miles. Normal water levels allow hikers to step across the dam here, using caution. From a trail junction on the east side of the dam, walk straight ahead on the Deer Hill Trail, passing the Leach Link trail where it departs left. Follow the path as it ascends steadily upward through mixed growth. You pull around to the southeast and then northeastward, passing through several clusters of white pine, birch, and low brush. The trail then turns southeast again for about a quarter mile on steeper grades. Soon you emerge in a pine grove beneath the Little Deer Hill

summit ledges at just under 1,100 feet in elevation, 1.25 miles from the road.

Views from the exposed stone here are outstanding. To the west is the striking procession of mountains that form the New Hampshire wall of the Cold River Valley, from Eastman Mountain in the south to Mount Meader and the Royce Mountains in the north. In the middle of the range you'll see the great, bare tops of North and South Baldface.

Look for the Deer Hill Trail as it continues northeast and east of Little Deer's summit in hardwoods. The path descends quickly into a slump, and then begins a meandering climb up Big Deer's west slope. You walk steadily upward now, the trail drifting southeast through some ledgy openings and then eastward again up more exposed rock in occasional stands of pitch pine. Some exposed rocky slabs here may be slippery in wet or icy weather. About 2 miles from your starting point, you crest a final rise and will find Big Deer's wooded 1,367-foot summit at a flat ledgy spot to the left of the trail. Continue southeast as the trail drops slightly and, in a short

CROSSING COLD RIVER

distance, arrive at an open ledge backed by pitch pines.

Here you have a fine outlook over Big Deer's hill-country neighbors to the southeast, including Pine, Lord, and Harndon Hills. Hike 27, the Conant Trail, will take you over these interesting peaks near Horseshoe Pond. Colton Hill is the distant 850-foot summit due south. The ledge here makes an excellent place to linger at roughly the midpoint of this hike.

Continue southwest on the Deer Hill Trail as it drops quickly toward its junction with the Deer Hill Bypass. The path follows the sheer south face of Big Deer through a series of openings with excellent views south and southwest. Use caution here, especially on wet ground. About a half mile below Big Deer's summit ledge, you reach a junction with the Deer Hill Bypass. The Deer Hill Trail you've been walking pulls left and south. You keep right on the bypass, walking northwest. Descending steadily, you reach an old mining road, and bear right, continuing generally to the northwest, going around and under the Little Deer ledges. You pass the Frost Trail on your right and shortly descend steeply west along an old stone wall. The path crosses more steeply angled ledge briefly and arrives at a grassy tote road, where you turn right and northwest. Follow the road along the river northward 0.4 miles to the site of the dam you crossed earlier. Walk over the dam to the west side of the Cold River again, turn right and north, walking the Deer Hill Connector back to the lot where you began this hike.

Note: At the time of writing (2016), old carry roads on the southwest side of these hills were being opened to very small-scale gem-mining operations. A new, rough gravel right-of-way touches the bypass as it descends. The junction may not be well-marked. Do not take this newer, rough gravel road to the southwest, but keep right on the Bypass.

During early spring snowmelt season, high water may prevent crossing the Cold River dam.

VIEWS TO THE CONANT TRAIL FROM BIG DEER

The Conant Trail: Pine Hill, Lord Hill, Harndon Hill

DISTANCE (AROUND CIRCUIT): 5.5 miles

HIKING TIME: 4 hours

VERTICAL RISE: 1,200 feet

MAPS: USGS 7.5′ Center Lovell, ME; USGS 15′ North Conway, NH; Chatham Trails Association Map of CTA Service Area; AMC Evans Notch map

The Conant Trail in Stow forms an elongated circuit over two 1,200-foot-plus mountains in the border country of western Maine. Like its neighbors, Big and Little Deer Mountains (see Hike 26), the Conant Trail lies at the south end of Evans Notch off a Maine road that meanders in and out of New Hampshire. At the most easterly point on the Conant Trail, there are some unique geological resources and striking views of beautiful Horseshoe Pond. This ramble through the unspoiled backcountry of the Cold River region makes a perfect day hike of moderate length.

The Conant Trail can be approached from east or west. From the west, drive south from Gilead or north from Fryeburg on ME 113. Turn east on a gravel road at a bridge over Chandler Brook. This bridge is 13.5 miles south of Gilead. Alternatively, it's 1.75 miles north of the junction of the north end of Chatham Loop Road and ME 113; or 0.5 mile south of the AMC Cold River Camp. The trailhead is 1.5 miles east of the point where you leave ME 113 in Stow.

From the east, you can approach the trailhead by taking gravel Deer Hill Road west from near the former inn buildings at Evergreen Valley in North Lovell, Maine, just off ME 5. The Conant trailhead is 4.8 miles west of the point where you hit the gravel road beyond the former Evergreen Valley resort area.

Coming from either direction, turn south at a big white pine with a small Chatham Trails Association (CTA) sign and drive in 50 yards from Deer Hill Road. Where another woods road comes in from your right, park out of the way on the grassy shoulder.

With some water and perhaps lunch in your rucksack, follow a woods road to the left (east), passing through a clearing

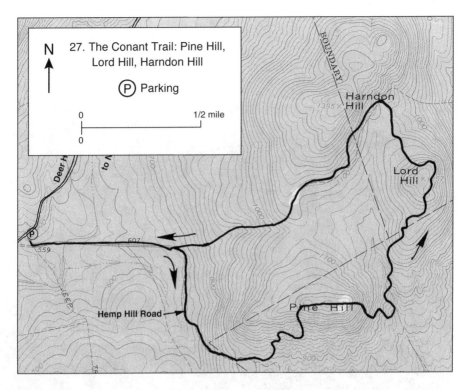

and over a causeway that bisects Colton Brook deadwater. A dam lies up to your right. Continue east and southeast on this stony gravel road, rising in beech, hemlock, red pine, and birch. You soon pass a small A-frame camp on your right and a stone house on your left. There are lovely, brushy stone walls on both sides of the road. You'll pass several grassy turnouts before the trail turns right (south) on another gravel track, known as Hemp Hill Road. This point marks the beginning and end of a circuit, roughly 5 miles in length, over Pine, Lord, and Harndon Hills. Watch for yellow blazes marking this turn. Wild sarsaparilla and bracken fern line Hemp Hill Road, along which you now walk to the south and southeast, rising gradually. Dip into a hollow, crossing a corrugated bridge over a small, seasonal brook, and, reentering national forest land, pass by a cutover area to your

right. Through the trees to your left are occasional good views of the impressive hanging cliffs on the west side of Pine Hill. The road narrows as it continues to rise southward through mature hemlock, oak, and spruce.

Roughly 0.75 mile from where you parked, watch for the old cellar holes of the long-abandoned Johnson farm, and bear immediately left as the trail leaves Hemp Hill Road. Passing another CTA sign, the path now climbs noticeably to the northeast in white pine groves dotted with beech and black oak. The route here runs over a disused tote road once used by twitch horses to pull out felled timber. Views begin to open up to the west as the trail climbs through a series of switchbacks. Pulling around to the north, you now make the steep scramble up to the final rise to the west ledges of Pine Hill.

THE VIEW NORTH FROM THE CONANT TRAIL

Once on the ledges, you have superb views over the Cold River Valley to the hills of the Evans Notch region and some of the major peaks in the Carter-Moriah Range in New Hampshire. In the distance, a few small farms dot the countryside. You may want to rest here a while, enjoying the scene. When you're ready to continue, climb farther eastward on moderate grades along the forested ridge of Pine Hill. The route here runs over several grassy hummocks through birch, oak, balsam, and spruce, then rises again to the more open main summit. Thick mats of moss and reindeer lichen-covered granite form a platform from which you'll enjoy good outlooks to the north. The tiny white flowers of mountain sandwort grow in the clearing. Another 10 minutes of walking along this pleasant ridge brings you to the east summit of Pine, with its fine

forestation has grown densely across the col. The trail drops farther through this zone and crosses pretty Bradley Brook. Look for views back to the ridge from which you just descended. Rise again to the east and cross a gravel road, reentering the woods, and climb Lord Hill northeastward through scattered clearings of low-bush blueberries, sweet fern, and bracken. In a few minutes you'll skirt the true summit of Lord Hill and emerge on the lovely, open ledges of this 1,257-foot mountain.

Below, to the east, you'll spot aptly named Horseshoe Pond, its two prongs running north and south around a peninsula. It's a pretty body of water, and the views to the mountains north and eastward around North Lovell are equally striking. Next, continue up the ledgy rise behind you toward the west and come at once to a junction where a side trail left will take you to the site of an old mineral dig. The largest gem-quality aquamarine and beryl crystals found in North America were uncovered here. This same potassium-feldspar ledge has been a chief source of topaz in Maine.

The Conant Trail heads right and away from the mine link, however, dropping quickly to the north toward Harndon Hill. Entering pine woods, you shortly come to a junction where a trail departs to the right for Horseshoe Pond. Keep left (northwest) at this point, walking through pretty corridors of pine as you head for Harndon Hill on a plateau 1,100 feet in elevation. Stone walls crop up here and there, a reminder that many years ago these hillsides were in pasture, the locations of remote hill farms. You'll cross grown-up old fields, now gone back to the wild in sweet fern, blueberries, and brush.

Roughly 0.5 mile below the Lord Hill ledges, the Conant Trail pulls to your

open ledge and excellent views toward Lord Hill and the mountain country to the northeast and east.

The path next drops quickly downward to the southeast, then turns back north and northeast toward Lord Hill. In the notch area between Pine and Lord Hills, you'll see the unmistakable work of the forester. About 30 years ago, these lands were "regeneration cut" to remove undesirable brush and undergrowth. New

left and begins its long march westward. The trail slabs along the side of Harndon Hill, but does not ascend to its summit. Work your way westward on a clear trail in mixed-growth forest, staying to the north of the regeneration forest cut to your left. The walking here is fairly level as you hike beside another stone wall under the brow of Harndon Hill. The fragrant smell of young balsam can be picked up on the air. White birches dot a hillside strewn with granite boulders. Another stone wall appears uphill on your right.

Soon you hike past the long-disused Harndon homesite, where the old foundation holes and a stone-walled corral are visible. A blueberry field lies beyond the weathered foundation stones. Like its neighbor, Lord Hill, Harndon Hill itself has been a source of fine gemstones, particularly topaz. You walk on to the west through a corner formed by intersecting stone walls, then bear to the southwest, descending steadily. The trail continues down amid black-berry brambles, then widens in hemlock woods dotted with violets. You're on what was Harndon Hill Road; this remnant of it provides easy walking westward.

A series of springs to your right soon becomes a brook that parallels this grassy road. Passing through a recovering clear-cut, the road widens further and you pass a 200-year-old cemetery. Though badly overgrown, hand-cut headstones and gate-stones can be seen. The thought of the families who settled here and made a stand against the mountain is a poignant one; their lives finished, the woods and brush have again taken over.

Continuing downhill, pass a woods road that runs off to your right, and soon come to the junction with Hemp Hill Road where you turned earlier. Proceed straight ahead and westward here and in a few minutes you will pass the two dwellings you saw earlier. Walking west still, cross the deadwater again and arrive at your parking place.

Ames and Speckled Mountains

DISTANCE (ROUND TRIP): 8.25 miles

HIKING TIME: 5 hours

VERTICAL RISE: 2,150 feet

MAPS: USGS 7.5′ Speckled Mountain, ME; USGS 7.5′ Wild River, NH; AMC Evans Notch map

At the southern end of Evans Notch stands a fine old brick country house, built in the mid-1800s. It is precisely the kind of place in which one would picture the hardiest of country types braving wild mountain winters. Certainly there was a time when such visions might have accurately reflected life hereabouts. Today, the building serves as headquarters for a Boy Scout council and is manned, in summers, to provide information. But the countryside here in the notch is as wild as ever. It is from the yard of the Brickett Place (as the old house is known) that you'll begin your ascent of Ames and Speckled Mountains.

You've room to park your car near the house, just off Evans Notch Road (ME 113), about 11 miles north of Stow. The Bickford Brook Trail leaves the east side of the house yard, and rises quickly southeast and east. At 0.3 mile, your route connects with the Speckled Mountain fire road and turns generally northeast toward the summits. The fire road is a rough grass-and-gravel way, once suitable only for the toughest of four-wheel-drive vehicles, and now closed to all vehicles, and often overgrown with scrub.

At the 0.5-mile mark, the trail levels off briefly, and the Blueberry Ridge Trail departs to your right. Continue up the Bickford Brook Trail, and at about 0.6 mile watch for a side path to your right, which will take you out to views of the sand-and-gravel slides that extend down into the Bickford Brook ravine. Just above this side path the fire road crosses several feeder brooks, one or two of which are good sources of water even in dry season.

Another short side trail to your right, just above here, leads to good upstream views of Bickford Brook and its falls.

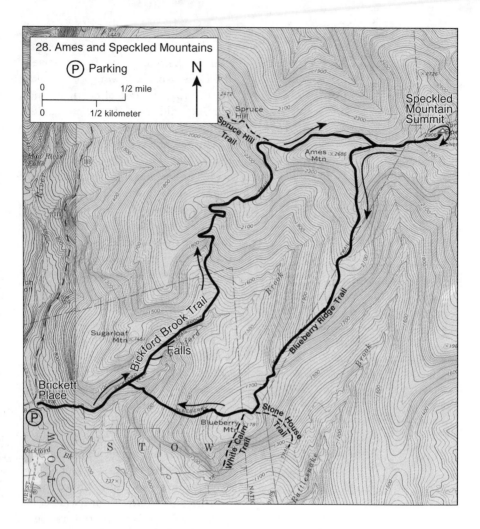

You'll get a closer view of the Upper Falls at lookouts just to the right of the trail at about the 1.25-mile mark. Listen for the roar.

After leveling off briefly, the trail climbs more steeply northeast, north, and northwest, making two S-curves between the Upper Falls and the 2.5-mile point. You climb steadily through the curves, rising up through beech, a belt of evergreens, and then mixed beech and yellow birch. Travel briefly west along the ridge, and, turning northeasterly again, walk down through a depression where the sunlight is filtered by densely grown balsams. The trail narrows in brushy terrain. It is hard to believe that two decades ago this path was wide enough to accommodate trucks and Jeeps.

At 2.75 miles, there are limited views of Mount Meader to the west. The Spruce Hill Trail enters from your left as you approach the 3-mile mark. Although you won't notice it, you'll pass the wooded summit of Ames Mountain in the next 0.25 mile as the trail slabs eastward toward the summit of Speckled Mountain. You'll get partial views

SPECKLED MOUNTAIN IN LATE WINTER

northward into Evans Notch here, as the path becomes rougher and more rutted.

At 3.5 miles, the Blueberry Ridge Trail appears on your right, just as you turn northeastward again for the final rise to the summit of Speckled Mountain. You climb fairly steeply here, past what used to be the last turnaround point for vehicles on the fire road, and move on to the rocky summit crowned by the site of the former fire tower.

The view from Speckled runs from northwest to southeast. The south side of the summit is wooded. What you can see is impressive anyway. East and West Royce Mountains are to the northwest in the foreground, and the Moriahs are just visible behind them and slightly northward. To the north, you can spot the Mahoosuc region; Goose Eye, in particular, stands out, as does Caribou Mountain (see Hike 32). Old Speck can be seen if conditions are right.

The horseshoe-shaped formation that is Butters, Red Rock, and Elizabeth Mountains lies to the east. Miles Notch is partly visible if you look to the easternmost end of the low range, where Elizabeth Mountain slopes southward. Looking southeast, you'll note two bodies of water: Virginia and Keewaydin Lakes.

If you return by the same route you climbed, the mountain provides an easy and quick descent. If you want to continue the loop, go down the Blueberry Ridge Trail. You leave the Bickford Brook Trail about 0.5 mile below the summit at the marker. Your new route turns left and continues southwesterly. The trail rises and falls over a series of slumps for 0.5 mile, sometimes in the open and sometimes under trees. You pass shortly over open ledges where you should watch carefully for cairns, indicating the route of travel. There are good views in a southerly direction from the ledges. To your left, down in the ravine, is Rattlesnake Brook.

Now on Blueberry Ridge, you descend with splendid views ahead of you. You reach a spring and then climb left to a junction with the Stone House Trail, approximately 2.5 miles below the summit. The Blueberry Ridge Trail turns right (westerly) at this point, passes a junction with the White Cairn Trail on your left, and descends westward to Bickford Brook. After descending for nearly a mile, cross Bickford Brook and continue west. Climbing the westerly side of the ravine, join Bickford Brook Trail again 0.9 mile from the Stone House Trail junction, and about 0.5 mile above the Brickett Place. Arriving shortly on the fire road again, turn left (south) here for the short walk out to Evans Notch Road and the Brickett Place.

29

East Royce Mountain

With a long enough arm, one could reach out from the summit of East Royce Mountain in Maine and touch New Hampshire air. No legerdemain is involved; it's just that East Royce is probably Maine's western-most elevation. The Maine–New Hampshire border falls between the two peaks of Royce Mountain, with the Maine—or eastern—peak rising imposingly by the center of majestic Evans Notch.

East Royce is not a mammoth mountain, given its immediate 4,000- to 6,000-foot neighbors, but from its 3,100-foot summit, it offers superb views of the Carter-Moriah Range and of the Presidentials beyond. East Royce also provides an excellent outlook to the lower summits to the east in Maine. To the south are North and South Baldface, Eagle Crag, Mount Meader, and the Basin.

The East Royce Trail entrance is well posted on Evans Notch Road (ME 113), about 3 miles north of the Brickett Place (see Hike 28) and Cold River Camp. There is room to leave your car in a grove at the trailhead just off the road on the west side.

The East Royce Trail is barely under way when it crosses the lower reaches of Evans Brook, a stream that begins up on the mountain and flows northerly into the Wild River and the Androscoggin at the head of the notch. After crossing the brook, climb first to your right, and then left (west), ascending the clearly defined track of an old logging road.

After about 650 feet, a water-worn granite ledge marks the second brook crossing. Your path now swings southwest up along the left bank. Continue along the logging road, paralleling the brook and climbing steadily through stands of tall hardwoods and mixed

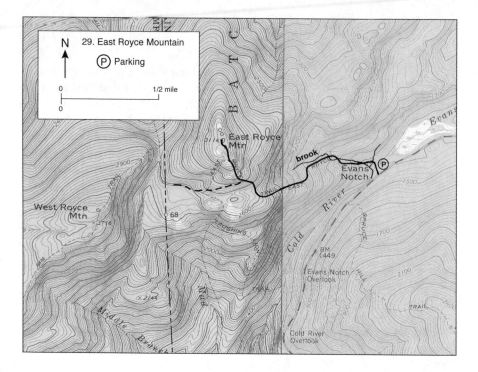

birch. Shortly before you reach the 0.5-mile point, cross the brook again, turning sharply right (watch for a small arrow on trees). The trail moves northwesterly here over to the main tributary of Evans Brook. In sight of Evans Falls (high on your right), the trail (you are still on the logging road) crosses a feeder brook, swings west again, and ascends an elevated rib of land between the two waterways.

Shortly after passing Evans Falls, the pathway crosses the feeder brook to your left, then continues right (westward) up through some fine silver birches as you near the 1-mile mark. Although the old logging road is easily picked out in this section, the brooks are dry in late summer. Brook crossings are less obvious. Watch carefully. The way here is bordered on both sides by handsome clusters of both white and silver birch.

The trail and logging road climb up a steep rise to what must have been a loading area for timber up on the ridge. Birches give way to evergreens here. On the ridge, continue westward and climb through some stone outcrops and low evergreens. The grade here becomes quite steep for about 0.5 mile. The trail levels off briefly about 1.25 miles from the road, where it joins the link to the summit and forms a connector to the Royce and Burnt Mill Brook Trails.

Approximately 0.25 mile below the summit, at the junction, a pronounced right turn to the north on a well-defined path begins the ascent of the open ledges that lie below the top. Watch for early southeasterly views framing Spruce Hill and Ames and Speckled Mountains. On the final leg to the top, follow painted blazes and cairns over the ledges to the northwest.

In spring, the summit view to the west reveals the Presidentials in fine

HIKING IN EVANS NOTCH

alpine garb, white with snow. The summit of Mount Washington is visible over West Royce and Zeta Pass, between South Carter and Mount Hight. South (and left) of Mount Hight is the distinctive shape of Carter Dome. Mount Madison lies west-northwest over North Carter. Adams, Jefferson, and Clay trail off to the west from Madison. Except for some low scrub that screens the view to the north and northeast, you can see in all directions here.

Pass from the south summit to the north crown by following the signs marking the path through the scrub. This short walk is worth the effort, as there are some splendid views to the north and east from the more northerly lookout.

In descending, follow the same route as you did coming up. Keep a cautious eye on the less prominent sections of the trail so you don't miss the turns and crossings. Sections of this trail have been relocated occasionally. Expect some changes as the trail climbs Braided Evans Brook.

30

Blueberry Mountain, Stone House–White Cairn Loop

DISTANCE (ROUND TRIP): 4.25 miles

HIKING TIME: 3 hours

VERTICAL RISE: 1,400 feet

MAPS: USGS 7.5′ Speckled Mountain, ME; USGS 7.5′ Wild River, NH; Chatham Trails Association area map; AMC Evans Notch map

The Stone House–White Cairn Loop over the south arm of Blueberry Mountain is arguably the prettiest walk in the Evans Notch region. Luckily, it's an easily accessible hike and, in the main, moderate enough in the demands it makes on the hiker to be open to all levels of ability. Nestled at the south end of Evans Notch, this approach to Blueberry Mountain lies between Deer Hill to the south and the higher summits of Ames and Speckled Mountains to the north.

Like most of the walks described in this area, the Stone House–White Cairn Loop is reached from ME 113, the Evans Notch Road, which can be picked up either in Fryeburg to the south or to the north in Gilead at its junction with US 2. Watch for Stone House Road on the east side of 113, 1.3 miles north of the AMC Cold River Camp. Head in on this dirt road by some mailboxes, pass through a cluster of cabins, and cross a wooden bridge over Bickford Brook. Immediately beyond the brook, the road bears to the right and then left, heading east again. You stay with this road for slightly more than 1 mile from the paved surface, and then park to the right just before a locked gate. Be sure to pull off the road so as not to block the gate.

The hike traverses the gravel road past the gate to the east as you walk through some pretty mixed growth and open field. In about 0.3 mile, you'll pass the White Cairn Trail on your left where it enters the road next to a couple of giant hardrock maples. Continue eastward, watching for the beginning of the Stone House Trail on your left, just beyond a small white outbuilding. The turn is well marked. Please respect the privacy of the Stone House owners by staying off the grounds, as requested.

The route now turns northeast over

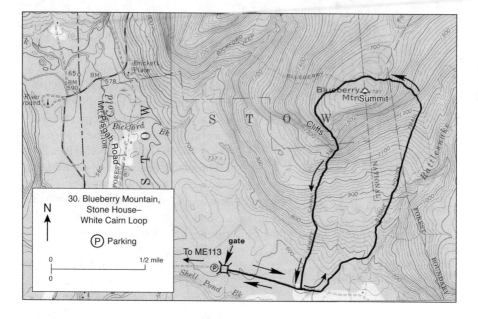

a winding logging road that sees occasional use. After several turns, the road passes Rattlesnake Brook Flume on your right. Take time to walk over to the stream, as the channel the water has chiseled through the granite is very much worth seeing. A footbridge also crosses the midpoint of the flume. Walking north on the trail again, find a sign pointing to Rattlesnake Pool via a side trail on your right. Take this side trail approximately 150 yards east to the pool and falls, which are even more attractive than the flume below. On a hot day, you may even be reluctant to move on.

Resuming your walk, return to the main trail and walk northward on the tote road through young beech. The route rises gradually but steadily here, and you pass through a grove of balsam just under 1 mile from where you parked. There has been timber harvesting in the area periodically, and in places the trail may be rough, obscured, or rerouted. Pulling slightly around to the northwest, walk next through more second-growth hard-

wood and bear left (west) as the trail leaves the tote road and heads for the summit. The route now becomes quite steep, and the real climbing in this hike takes place in this section.

Norway spruce form an arch over the closely grown trail as you move upward (west). Shortly, the trail climbs onto the open ledges of the summit. The Blueberry Ridge Trail comes in on your right; follow it straight ahead across the broad summit. The highest point on the mountain is marked by a cairn where the Summit Loop Trail begins. This is a good place to rest and enjoy the views to the north over Ames and Speckled Mountains (see Hike 28).

The Summit Loop Trail should be passed up in favor of a walk to the west ledges where the Blueberry Ridge Trail starts downhill. You'll have to cover this ground anyway, heading for the White Cairn trailhead. Just continue to the west over the summit, dropping briefly into a wooded, boggy depression, and then out onto more granite. A sign indi-

LOOKING WEST FROM THE SUMMIT OF BLUEBERRY MOUNTAIN

cates the White Cairn Trail on your left. Just ahead there are splendid views to the west and northwest from East and West Royce Mountains down to Mount Meader and the Baldfaces. On a clear fall day with the sun in the west, there are few nicer spots in Evans Notch than right here.

Backtracking a little, uphill, bear right (south) on the White Cairn Trail, which marches toward the lower end of the Notch over more red pine-studded ledges. Walk southwest and south, descending quickly in the open. In 0.25 mile you emerge on more attractive ledges with spectacular views over a sheer drop to the southwest, south, and southeast. Deer Hill lies due south, with Harndon Hill and Styles Mountain more around to the southeast and east. Shell Pond is the body of water to the southeast. The trail skirts the edge of the ledges, keeping this panorama in front of you, and then pulls to the east through a stand of white oak. Use caution here and below. The descent is steep.

The trail drops down to the south abruptly, runs through a grove of red pine, and then drops sharply again to the west. More on the level now, you meander to the south, crossing several logging roads that come in from various angles. Be careful not to get sidetracked here. The trail passes through a stand of tall, spindly balsams and then descends to a low, boggy point where it is crossed by another logging road. It is only another 100 yards before you emerge on the gravel road. Bear right for the brief walk back to the gate and your car.

Albany Mountain

DISTANCE (ROUND TRIP): 3.8 miles	
HIKING TIME: 3 hours	
VERTICAL RISE: 1,100 feet	
MAP: USGS 7.5' East Stoneham, ME	

Well off by itself and nestled in a cluster of other low summits, Albany Mountain in Albany, Mason, and Stoneham is a gem of a hike several miles south of West Bethel. Near pretty Crocker Pond, the mountain lies in those 46,000 acres of the White Mountain National Forest (WMNF) that are on the Maine side of the border with New Hampshire. Albany can be done as a day-hike, or as an overnighter, tenting before or after the hike at Crocker Pond campground. (Call WMNF for campsite reservations.)

To reach the trailhead, take US 2 west from Bethel or east from Gilead and turn south on Flat Road opposite the West Bethel post office. Follow Flat Road south for 5.5 miles, then turn right on Crocker Pond Road, which leads to the trail and campground. WMNF signs for hiking and camping mark this turn. Travel a short distance along the campground road, and watch for the Albany Notch trailhead and parking area on the right at 6.2 miles. (If you are camping at Crocker Pond, it's a good idea to leave your car there and walk the 0.8 miles back to the trailhead.)

From the trail board, walk west and southwest on easy grades as the Albany Notch Trail heads toward the mountain and Albany Notch. The trail rises slowly in protected forest on an old tote road. Soon the route departs abruptly left to higher ground capped by hemlocks, bypassing a wet section, rejoining the road in minutes. Five little seasonal brooks are crossed in rolling terrain as you continue southwest. About 0.4 miles into the woods, the trail reaches a sizable bog, which has often been held captive by beavers who dam feeder streams of New England Brook. Periodically, WMNF personnel remove the dams, and the trail should be passable here.

Turn left at the edge of the bog (arrow)

and walk south a short distance, crossing a spit of grassy ground to the southwest. This indistinct footpath takes you over a couple of wet spots and emerges on a new trail to the southwest in deciduous forest. This terrain supports silver birch and is dotted with glacial erratics. The path proceeds upward to the southwest where it runs to the right of a low stone wall, and ascends over several sets of stone steps and impoundments. You walk more to the south and southeast next, this new route pulling still farther away from the old notch trail, which was frequently wet and boggy. A younger forest of beech, ash, oak, and other hardwoods dominate the walk. Rising more steeply southwestward, the

path crosses several more small brooks and then follows another, which lies to the right in a depression. Runoff has created a weave of intertwined brooks here, and in places the trail itself becomes part of this. You meander south and southwest, rising noticeably now, the trail bordered with mosses, lycopodium, and low scrub.

The trail pulls west-northwest briefly by a large rock shelf draped in sphagnum moss, and then pulls southwest again over a stretch of rooted, rocky ground. Gradually, the grade slackens a bit, and the path narrows as hardwoods give way to tightly grown conifers, mainly red spruce and balsam. You soon enter the first of several openings with

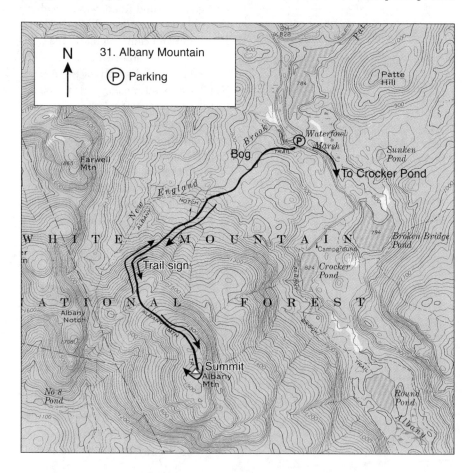

LOOKING NORTHWEST FROM ALBANY MOUNTAIN

patches of exposed ledge beneath as the trail turns to the southeast and east. The path becomes more obscure in blueberry bushes and low scrub, arriving at a trail marker 1.5 miles from the road. Turn left and southeast here to walk the remaining 0.4 mile to Albany's summit.

Pulling southeast again, the trail levels, passing over more exposed patches of granodiorite laced with quartzite. You reach a larger open spot now where a big boulder lies to the left of the trail. Look to your right (west) where two small stone cairns mark an opening in the woods. Take this side path a few dozen yards west to a splendid outlook with mountain views. Perhaps twenty peaks stand to the west, with all the higher summits around Evans Notch visible. To the northwest, over Peter Mountain,

you can just see a few of the summits of the Mahoosuc Range. Extensive strands of rhodora flourish here on the ledges.

Regaining the path to the summit, you head east-southeast over ledge amid more ground blueberry. As the trail approaches the summit, the climb becomes steeper where the path pulls west up the rib and then turns south again. Views begin to open up where there are breaks in the scrub as you arrive shortly on the summit plateau. You'll find a brushy, wooded summit but excellent views from open spaces, especially to the southeast and south. Walk farther south once on top to find these openings.

The path runs over a series of ribs, through a white pine grove, and pulls eastward through a stand of pitch pines. Leveling off, the trail arrives at an open, east-facing lookout. Here there are grand views toward Mount Abram to the northeast and a dozen lower summits to its south. You'll find numerous spots here to pause, rest, and take in the 180-degree sightlines.

Albany's true, wooded summit lies about fifty yards up the ledgy rise to the south, marked by a larger cairn. The summit zone supports an interesting copse of pitch pine. Here the species is near the absolute northern limit of its range. Another excellent lookout with views south toward Rattlesnake Mountain and Keewaydin Lake lies beyond the Summit cairn. Continue past the cairn and walk south on the path for a few minutes to reach this point.

If you move around through the summit scrub, you'll get glimpses of the many hills that surround Albany Mountain. To the immediate east are Bell and Square Dock Mountains, and, beyond them, Lovejoy, Cummings, and Peabody Mountains. To the immediate south lie Keewaydin Lake and Rattlesnake Mountain. On the southeast is Kneeland Pond, fed by Albany Brook. To the west, beyond Albany Notch, are Butters, Red Rock, Durgin, and Speckled Mountains. At the foot of Isaiah Mountain is Virginia Lake. Songo Pond is seen off to the northeast under Emery Hill.

Albany's summit supports plentiful blueberry growth in high summer, and, should you arrive at the right time, you

EXPLORING ALBANY'S SUMMIT

THE VIEW WEST FROM ALBANY MOUNTAIN

can pick to your heart's content, assuming others haven't had the same idea. Albany's summit ledges make a good place to linger and eat lunch, too.

The round trip from the trail board to Albany's eastern lookout near the summit requires about three hours of walking at a moderate pace. Allow extra time if you visit the southeastern lookout and the western lookout mentioned earlier.

32

Caribou Mountain

DISTANCE (AROUND LOOP): 7 miles

HIKING TIME: 5 hours

VERTICAL RISE: 1,900 feet

MAP: USGS 7.5′ Speckled Mountain, ME; AMC Evans Notch map

Often, the rewards offered by a mountain are tied to the seasons; some mountains are best climbed at certain times of the year. Caribou Mountain, for instance, deserves your attention in late spring and early summer. Get yourself up into Evans Notch while the last of the snow is still melting, and you're in for something special. Two fine waterways border the trails that form the Caribou loop. Before the warm weather sets in, these streams are running full tilt. They carry the snowmelt down the mountain alongside the trail. And in mid-May, there are few places in Maine I'd rather be.

Morrison Brook and the Caribou Trail interweave nearly to the summit. Along the way, there are some truly scenic cataracts and falls. On the return loop, Mud Brook forms high on the south ridges of Caribou opposite Haystack Mountain, and sticks close to Mud Brook Trail all the way out to the Notch Road. Together, the two brooks offer plenty of incentive to hike up Caribou and back, with the fine views from the top providing a special bonus.

The Caribou and Mud Brook Trails leave the east side of Evans Notch Road (ME 113) roughly 6.5 miles north of the Brickett Place and 6.25 miles south of the ME 113–US 2 intersection in Gilead. This new US Forest Service parking area is by the trailhead on the east side of the road. On the ascent, you leave the road and bear left, heading north and northwest parallel to the road. You walk more than 0.5 mile before bearing to the right, crossing Morrison Brook and working northeast and east toward Caribou Mountain. This is your first glimpse of a stream that you will rejoin shortly and that you will stay with most of the way to the summit.

Now, proceeding east-southeast, you soon cross the brook again and climb along the east side of the stream. You'll cross several feeder brooks here as they flow in from your right. At slightly over 1 mile, you'll note rows of very tall, old silver and yellow birch. Birches of this size and vintage are uncommon.

Heading due east, you climb steadily now, slabbing along the increasingly steep rise to the right of the trail. Morrison Brook flows at the bottom of the ravine to your left. As you look down from above, the brook makes a pretty sight—particularly if you've come at the right time of year.

From 0.25 to 2 miles along the trail, you walk above a series of cataracts and falls. Kees Falls is seen just past the 1.5-mile point, with another cascade (high and to the right of the trail) not far beyond.

Crossing Morrison once more and continuing eastward, you ascend more rapidly now as the trail hugs the left side of the ravine. Good views to the south and southwest emerge, especially if you're climbing in early spring or late autumn. Cross the last feeder brooks that flow into Morrison at about 2.5 miles from the road. The trail levels off briefly above here. Climbing again, you reach the col between Caribou and Gammon Mountains (there has been some blowdown here in recent years). The Caribou Trail continues straight ahead to Bog Road and West Bethel. Turn right here on the col and ascend Mud Brook Trail to the summit, traveling south and then southwest.

Continuing south, climb rapidly through birch and balsam to the first of two open summits beyond where you just turned. Proceed past the first clearing, which has views only to the northwest, and you'll arrive shortly at

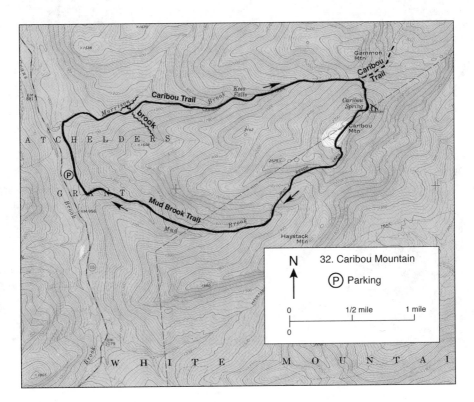

MORRISON BROOK ALONG THE CARIBOU TRAIL

the true summit, which boasts a fine 360-degree view.

Speckled Mountain is the most prominent summit immediately to the south-southwest. Slightly to the left, you see the upper reaches of Kezar Lake and Horseshoe Pond. East Royce Mountain lies across Evans Notch to the southwest. Behind Royce, stretching south to north on the far western horizon, lies the Carter-Moriah Range, topped by Mount Washington, still more distant. Peabody and Pickett Henry Mountains are to the immediate north. If you look between the two on a clear day, you'll see Old Speck far to the north.

To begin your descent via the second half of the Caribou loop, follow the cairns south to an open, lower ledge, where the views to the south and west continue to be excellent, but become more sheltered. The trail meanders over the ledge, briefly turns sharply eastward, and then resumes its course toward the south and southwest through mixed scrub. Watch the cairns carefully as you descend the ledges; it's easy to miss the trail here.

You'll turn westerly, rapidly descending amid tangled scrub and then through birch and balsam groves. At slightly less than 1 mile from the summit (2.5 miles above the road), the trail crosses two feeder streams that will shortly become Mud Brook—certainly a misnomer, for Mud Brook flows clear and clean from its origins to Evans Brook.

Beyond the streams, the trail proceeds west and northwest, slabbing the side of a ridge opposite Haystack Moun-

tain. There are good views to the south here. The gradual descent continues, as you drop down among tall hardwoods and then walk southwesterly through stands of birch and balsam again. More feeder brooks are crossed (you are now about midway on the trail), after which a steep southerly drop leads you across the brook again. Skirting the west ridge of Caribou, the walkout travels in a northwesterly direction with Mud Brook now on your left.

The final descent is gradual, and you pass through areas cut over for timber years ago. The route follows a logging road that intersects periodically with others, leaving open areas that have become deer pastures. Signs of deer are usually plentiful hereabouts, and you may be fortunate enough to spot a family of whitetails as they come down to the brook at sunset.

You'll keep close to the brook as the trail nears Evans Notch Road. Mud Brook meanders to the south in a wide loop below thick firs and momentarily away from the trail. The trail pulls to the right (north) in a recently relocated section, and makes its way to the parking area where you left your car on the right side of Evans Notch Road.

Recently, Caribou Mountain and the surrounding woodlands have been granted a wilderness designation by the federal government. This classification will protect the "backcountry" flavor of these grounds and preserve them, unchanged, for hikers visiting in future years.

33

The Roost

DISTANCE (ROUND TRIP AROUND LOOP, INCLUDING RETURN VIA NOTCH ROAD): 1.7 miles

HIKING TIME: 1 hour

VERTICAL RISE: 440 feet

MAP: USGS 7.5' Speckled Mountain, ME; AMC Evans Notch map

There is a kind of justice to mountain climbing: The excellence of the views you get at the top is often proportionate to the amount of effort expended in climbing up. Occasionally there are comfortable exceptions; the Roost is one of them.

The Roost is a small outcrop of ledge, a low summit, at the head of Evans Notch, offering good views south, west, and north. And it's all to be had for an easy climb. Indeed, there are many higher summits in Maine that provide fewer good outlooks. The Roost is an undemanding hike that will suit walkers who don't wish to tackle the Notch's higher peaks.

The Roost Trail begins in the township of Hastings on ME 113 (Evans Notch Road), about 3 miles south of US 2. A spacious camping area lies just south on the Notch Road. (Park off the road, south of the bridge, at Hastings Campground or at a WMNF area to the right, below the bend in the Wild River.) The trailhead is located at the junction of the Wild River and Evans Brook, and a more appealing prospect would be hard to imagine. The brook stretches southeasterly toward the Roost and Caribou Mountain, while the Wild River curves upstream and westward toward its origins high in Perkins Notch at Ketchum Pond.

Starting from ME 113 at the north end of Evans Brook Bridge, ascend the Roost Trail directly up a steep, low ridge. Climbing northeasterly, you reach level ground briefly above the ridge, then turn easterly toward the Roost. Your route is through hardwood groves, with several giant old white pines rising close to the trailside. This area was most likely cut over many years ago, with mixed-growth climax forest now present. At 0.25 mile, you cross a small

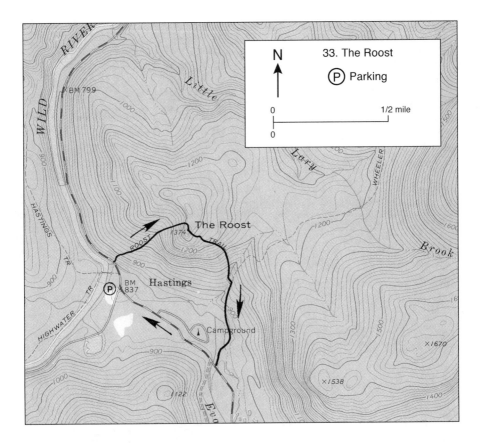

brook entering from your left. You'll see a giant boulder here to the right of the trail. Climbing through tall white birch, pass a low rock outcrop on your right, and then turn southward into a ledge depression surrounded by balsam and pine growth. This is the first of two ledges that form the Roost. A few yards southwest beyond this point, you'll emerge onto the true Roost, well above Evans Notch Road.

This nearly 1,400-foot-high ledge gives you an excellent view through the notch. East and West Royce Mountains rise well to the southwest, across the notch. Howe Peak stands directly opposite your position. Behind Howe Peak, the Moriahs stand out. Look to the far left (southeast) for Caribou Mountain. To the northwest, Baldcap and lower summits

lead northeast to Mahoosuc Notch. If the sun is with you, the ledges are a fine spot to rest and take in the view.

From here, there are two routes back to the road and your starting point. You can simply retrace your steps, and arrive back at the trailhead in about 20 minutes. Or you can continue a loop that descends gradually from the south, or far end, of the clearing. This route runs southeast and south, steps over a seasonal brook, eventually coming around to the southwest and emerging on ME 113 alongside a stream and north of the woods road that runs in toward Wheeler Brook. Turn right and north on ME 113, passing the Hastings Campground on your right, and you'll return in minutes to your starting place about 0.5 miles north.

VI.

THE MAHOOSUCS AND GRAFTON NOTCH

Mount Carlo–Goose Eye Circuit

DISTANCE (AROUND CIRCUIT): 7.8 miles

HIKING TIME: 5 hours

VERTICAL RISE: 1,800 feet

MAPS: USGS 7.5′ Gilead, ME; USGS 15′ Old Speck Mountain, ME; USGS 7.5′ Shelburne, NH; USGS 15′ Milan, NH

The Mahoosuc Range straddles the Maine–New Hampshire border, a collection of several exposed, higher summits in remote country, little-settled and wild. Maine uplands in this region are perhaps the more isolated and are mainly accessible via old logging roads from the New Hampshire side via Berlin or from above Grafton Notch in Maine.

Thousands of acres in this region have been part of paper-making empires, now more quiescent. The avenue of approach to the whole range and to this hike, itself a pulpwood highway, is Success Pond Road, entered from either Berlin (described here) or from Grafton Notch. This rough gravel road parallels the entire west side of the Mahoosuc Range. Hikers use Success Pond Road

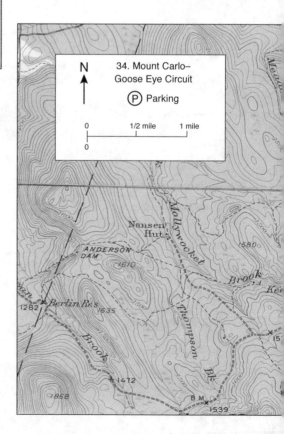

as a point of entry for a number of challenging climbs in the Mahoosucs, one of which is this exceptional circuit of two unique mountains, each over 3,500 feet in elevation.

Travel to Berlin, NH, to reach this hike. Cross the Androscoggin River at the north end of Main Street and turn into Hutchins Street, which loops to the left, crosses a railroad spur and pulls north, skirting paper mill pulp yards. Success Pond Road is a gravel way that continues to the northeast here. Follow Success Pond Road for 8.5 miles to the trailhead on the right. Parking is available just beyond the trailhead. Be sure to park well off the road as heavy logging trucks use this route.

Enter the Carlo Col Trail, cross a brook, and walk east on a signed gravel road for 0.2 mile to a trail junction. Here the Goose Eye Trail drops left. Continue eastward on the tote road, the Carlo Col Trail rising through a cutover area. (Timber and pulpwood harvesting continues at various points in this area. Expect the possibility of minor trail rerouting.) At 0.6 miles, the tote road divides, and you keep left, descending for a short distance and crossing Stearns Brook (use caution). There are occasional limited views of Carlo Col above and ahead in this section.

Climbing eastward, the path pulls to the right, avoiding more cutover ground. At just over a mile from the road, the trail runs along Stearns Brook for a short distance, crosses the brook briefly, and then crosses the brook again to its north side. Moose live in and

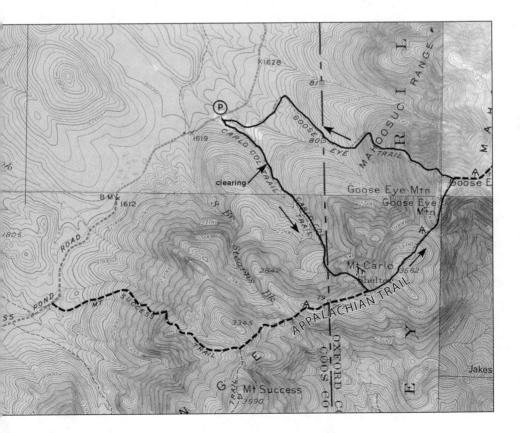

move through this landscape, and you will likely see their tracks and scat as you ascend. At just under two miles the route pulls away from the logged areas and climbs more steeply southeast toward the col. About 2.25 miles from the road you continue up along a small brook and pass a short link on the left that serves the Carlo Col shelter site. There is tenting space here at an elevation just below 3,000 feet. Continue upward, crossing the brook, and reach the cleft that marks the junction of the Carlo Col Trail and the Mahoosuc Trail

GOOSE EYE MOUNTAIN, MAHOOSUC RANGE

(AT) at 2.7 miles. Turn left and north here and ascend the ridgeline for 0.4 mile to the open 3,560-foot summit of Mount Carlo, where hikers have excellent views in several directions.

Eastward lies thousands of acres of unsettled country, historically logged as a part of paper company lands. To the far west are the mountains of the Kilkenny Range and Mount Cabot and, to the southwest, the Presidential Range, with its dozen imposing summits. Around to the north stands the distinctive shape of Goose Eye, toward which you now proceed.

Walk north from Carlo's summit, shortly reaching a little, flat clearing carpeted by sedge. It's a good spot to pause and perhaps eat lunch. If you do, expect to be visited by persistent Canada jays, who have come to associate the arrival of hikers with gourmet dining. These "whisky jacks," as they are sometimes called, will happily eat whatever is on offer from your hand. They will come back for seconds, too. The Mahoosuc Trail (AT) next rises over and around two crowns, enters a slight depression, and then rises steeply to a junction with the Goose Eye Trail 1.8 miles north of where you turned left on the AT. Bear left and west here, and, scrambling up the ledges of Goose Eye's bare west peak, you'll shortly reach its 3,870-foot summit.

Goose Eye offers another feast of views. To the north you can see sections of the AT as it follows the ridgeline to the northeast, with Old Speck and Baldpate looming in the far distance, beyond Mahoosuc Notch. Grand views of New Hampshire's Presidential Range are to the southwest with Mount Carlo in the foreground. One could spend a pleasant afternoon on this rock pile, identifying and counting mountains in all directions. The origin of the name "Goose Eye" isn't certain. Many suggestions exist, perhaps the most persuasive claiming that the mountain was "Goose high" as to altitude. Common spoken usage may have modified and passed the name along as Goose Eye to the present. Make up your own yarn.

When the valley beckons, look for the Goose Eye Trail, which descends to the west on steep, ledgy terrain. Don't try shortcuts here. Stay on the path, which skirts the most challenging outcrops of the ledge and then pulls left and west along an arm of the mountain, descending in tightly grown spruce scrub. The trail now plateaus briefly and then resumes its steep descent, pulling around to the northwest. At 1.2 miles below Goose Eye's summit, you walk down into stands of hardwoods as the trail pulls sharply southwest for less than a quarter mile and then turns northwest again on relaxed grades.

At 1.3 miles above Success Pond Road you cross into New Hampshire and continue downward, crossing a faint woods road and walking through a boggy area. Watch for trail signs carefully as you proceed through an area of tall grass and into a cutover. Pulling more to the right you emerge onto a gravel road and follow it for a short distance. Watch for route markers and turn to the left in woods cleared earlier and presently coming back in scrub. The path, now running south and southwest, crosses two brooks on nearly level ground and then proceeds to a rise. At the top of the short rise you come again to the junction with the Carlo Col Trail you passed as you ascended. Bear right and west here and, in 0.2 miles, arrive at Success Pond Road.

35

Old Speck

DISTANCE (ROUND TRIP): 7.5 miles

HIKING TIME: 6 hours

VERTICAL RISE: 2,730 feet

MAPS: USGS 15′ Old Speck Mountain, ME; USGS 15′ Milan, NH; AMC Mahoosuc Range map

Maine's third highest mountain (after Katahdin and Sugarloaf) will give you something to sink your teeth into. Old Speck provides the kind of hiking experience that lets you know you're in Maine. The mountain rises high over Grafton Notch and is reached via ME 26 from Bethel. Overnight camping is available on a first-come, first-served basis at Grafton Notch. Inquire at the parking lot trailboard or call WMNF.

The trail system on the mountain and in the notch has undergone some changes, and you should be aware that old maps may not have an accurate picture of available routes up the mountain. The Old Speck Trail, once known as the Fire Warden's Trail, now runs slightly north of the old route, and begins at a parking area on ME 26 a bit less than 3 miles north of Screw Auger Falls and about 12 miles northwest of Bethel. The old, badly eroded fire warden's route is no longer in use. The "new" Old Speck Trail includes parts of the former Cascade Brook Trail, the Eyebrow Trail, the Upper Ridge Link Trail, and the Skyline Trail. The route is clearly marked and there is a map of the route on a trail board at the parking area. The Old Speck Trail is the current route of the Appalachian Trail.

From the north side of the parking area, the Old Speck Trail runs west nearly on the level, bears left at a fork where the Eyebrow Trail comes in from the right, and climbs easily in the direction of the summit. Heading south-southwest, you cross Cascade Brook. Several feeder brooks are soon passed. Turn around to the north, slabbing the ridge as the trail runs through the first of two north-south S-curves. Passing close to the lower cascades on your right, proceed southwest again, then turn north through the second S, and head west, rising quickly to the left of the cascades.

The upper reaches of the brook are followed to approximately the 0.75-mile point, where the trail turns sharply right, crosses the brook, and moves northward along ledges toward the Eyebrow. There are excellent views down the valley in this section. The ledges are steep and sometimes wet. Cable hand rolls are mounted. Use caution here.

To continue toward the summit, follow the Old Speck Trail through an evergreen grove north and northwest, then swing west up the ridge to the uneven timberline. At 1.5 miles, open spaces provide views of the summit approximately 2.25 miles away. A long ridge walk takes you through forests of red spruce, over a series of hummocks and bare ledges.

At 0.75 miles below the summit, pass the Link Trail down to the site of the old fire warden's cabin. The Old Speck Trail dips into a final depression before rising sharply to a junction with the Mahoosuc Trail, which runs right to Speck Pond. Turn left here and, passing the disused old Fire Warden's Trail on your left, arrive in about 0.25 miles at the 4,180-foot summit.

A rebuilt observation tower on the summit is worth a careful climb, for the views run 360 degrees and are outstanding. You can look to the southwest directly down Mahoosuc Notch,

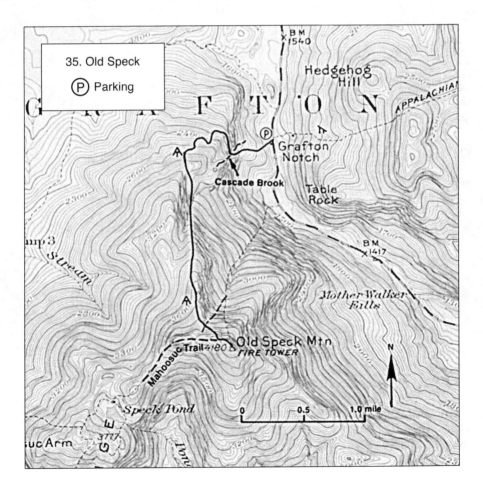

THE NORTHEAST ARM OF OLD SPECK

OLD SPECK VIEWED FROM THE EAST

framed by Mahoosuc and Fulling Mill Mountains. The twin peaks of Baldpate rise strikingly to the northeast; Dresser and Long Mountains are due east; Slide Mountain and Sunday River Whitecap are to the southeast. On a clear day, if you look beyond Baldpate, the mountains of the Rangeley region—particularly Saddleback— stand out. There is plenty of room on the wooded summit to stretch out or prepare lunch, and you may encounter a large, friendly rabbit with whom I've had several one-sided conversations.

Make the return trip by retracing your steps to ME 26. Use caution when descending, especially on ledge and in wet areas around the cascades.

36

Table Rock, Baldpate Mountain

DISTANCE (ROUND TRIP): 2.8 miles (via Appalachian Trail and Table Rock upper side trail)

HIKING TIME: 2 hours, 30 minutes

VERTICAL RISE: 900 feet

MAP: USGS 15' Old Speck Mountain, ME; AMC Mahoosuc Range map

Baldpate is a great, two-peaked mountain on the east side of Grafton Notch in western Maine. Its east-west mass carries the Appalachian Trail (AT) for over 10 miles, provides a shelter off the AT near its west peak, and is host to Table Rock on its southwest side. Table Rock is part of a series of ledges, fractured rock, and tumulus that form a wall with brilliant outlooks over Grafton Notch and Old Speck. The rock can be ascended from its base to the southwest or reached via the AT and a side trail from Grafton Notch. It can also be done as a challenging loop (see page 171). Here we describe the approach from the AT and return.

From Bethel, drive north on US 2, ME 5, and ME 26, bearing left on ME 26 (Bear Notch Road) in Newry. Continue northwest and west on ME 26 through North Newry, pass Step Falls, and enter Grafton Notch State Park. You may wish to pause and examine Screw Augur Falls and Mother Walker Falls on the left, where the notch rock has been sculpted by centuries of falling water. Beyond these sites, proceed to a parking area on the left that serves Old Speck and Baldpate hikers where the AT crosses Route 26. Look for the trail board here where you'll find notices and local maps.

From this location, walk northeast and right a few dozen yards on the AT to where it crosses ME 26. Across the road, follow the white-blazed AT northeast and east through a low area of white-paper birches and shortly cross a pretty little brook. At a "Y," you pass the orange-blazed lower side trail to Table Rock on the right. Continue east and northeast as the AT climbs in the direction of Baldpate's distant west peak. Stands of young hardwoods, including maple and beech, line the trail. Grades begin to steepen

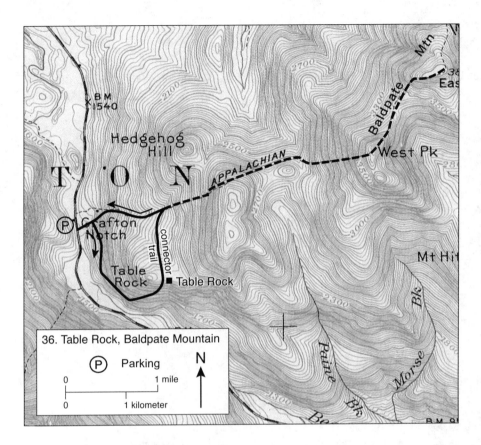

36. Table Rock, Baldpate Mountain

(P) Parking   N

0   1 mile

0   1 kilometer

as you meander upward over numerous tangles of roots, loose stone, and exposed pavement. You pass by a dozen or so glacial erratics on either side of the trail as the path pulls to the southeast and then around to the east again.

Roughly 0.6 miles above the road, you cross a stream and pool, both lodged in a rock-strewn channel. Tree cover changes now, more balsam, hemlock, and spruce grow here as you ascend into a cooler climate zone. Walk over an extended patch of exposed stone pavement soon, where it's easy to see how thin the ground cover is on these rocky Maine mountains. About 0.9 miles above ME 26, you reach the upper side trail to the Table Rock ledges. Turn right and south here, leave the AT, and walk this interesting, blue-blazed side trail for a half mile to where the densely grown woods open up above the ledges.

The path levels off briefly, and you cross a couple of low sections with stone steps as the trail turns briefly to the southwest and west. Climb up a set of stone steps as the route leans southward again, and go through a little glade and along a boardwalk. Passing through a thick band of low deciduous scrub, you ascend another stone stairway. Descending slightly, you step over the two threads of a brook. The trail rises gradually again to the south in thickets of balsam and spruce, climbs over another stone staircase, and passes a large boulder. A half mile from where you left the AT, you go through a narrow

SEVEN AUGUR FALLS, GRAFTON NOTCH

RELAXING AMONG STUNNING VIEWS, TABLE ROCK

corridor of scrub and ascend straight up a nearly vertical rockfall. Use caution.

You arrive now at a great pluton of rock, part of the Table Rock capstone, which you climb to on steel ladder rungs. Walk a short distance through a grove of conifers and note, on your left, where the lower Table Rock (orange blazes) trail comes up through a steep cleft. Step westward and emerge on the large, open expanse of "The Table." The exposed rock below stretches southwest along the mountain, and there are splendid views from almost anywhere atop this wall of stone. Table Rock is a kind of tabletop, its "legs" many varied supporting sections of layered cliff. The Table affords stunning views down Grafton Notch, across to the great, brooding mass of Old Speck, Maine's fourth-highest summit, and to nearby cliffs and subsidiary mountains. To the southeast are limited views of distant Puzzle Mountain. Sunday River White-cap and Slide Mountain lie to the south, adjacent to Old Speck. Also due south, you can see down the long valley below the notch, which you drove up ear-

lier. Dozens of other, lower mountains stand to the south and southeast as far as the eye can see. On this perch, you are in the heart of Maine's high border country.

When it's time to head down, carefully return to the upper side trail you walked earlier. Descending carefully, walk north on the side trail 0.5 miles back to the AT junction where you turned before. At the junction, bear left on the AT and descend 0.9 miles to ME 26. Once across the road, walk the short distance left and south to the parking area.

AN ALTERNATIVE APPROACH TO TABLE ROCK

For those who might prefer a more challenging hike to Table Rock, there is an alternative route that turns the previous description on its head. It is appropriate only for those who are fit, have reasonable upper body strength, and who are comfortable on exposed heights. You should also be accompanied by another experienced hiker due to the various

PROFILE OF TABLE ROCK CLIFFS OVER ME 26

challenges in this route—a helping hand and leg up will be much appreciated in several places. To ascend by this Maine Bureau of Public Lands route, cross ME 26 as noted earlier. Once into the woods on the AT, bear right and south on the first orange-blazed side path, the Table Rock Trail. Follow this trail southeast as it slabs the hillside to its left above a wet, boggy depression. In 0.6 miles you reach the beginning of a series of esses, after which the trail drops into a pronounced ravine. Climbing out of this cleft, you pull right and soon reach the first opening on this trail at .8 miles from the trailhead, where there are views. Advancing upward steadily, the trail gradually works its way around the base of the ledges that rise here and reaches a series of rock caves. Several are found along this cliff face. (Entering these caves can be hazardous and is not recommended.) The route now moves entirely over rock, from boulder to slab,

and, in several places, handholds may be necessary. Some sections are quite steep and demand good coordination. Approaching Table Rock, climb a short, steep cleft in the cliff rocks to reach a junction with the upper side trail. Turn left and emerge on Table Rock, where the outstanding views mentioned before are seen. To descend, completing a loop, take the blue-blazed upper Table Rock side trail described earlier, where a 0.5 mile walk north brings you to the AT. At the junction with the AT, turn left and west, walking down in 0.9 miles to the parking lot on ME 26.

The ascent via the cliff face on the Table Rock Trail isn't recommended in wet or icy weather and, again, is only suitable for experienced, fit hikers. Descending via the lower Table Rock Trail is not recommended. Add 30 to 45 minutes to the total time for this hike if you choose to ascend via the lower Table Rock Trail and then descend via the AT.

VII.

MOUNT DESERT ISLAND–ACADIA NATIONAL PARK

MOUNT DESERT ISLAND

Mount Desert is the largest coastal island in Maine. Its kidney-shaped land mass lies off Trenton at the head of Frenchman Bay, east of Blue Hill and west of Schoodic Point. A heavily glaciated, mountainous island, Mount Desert makes a spectacular destination for the hiker. Clearly marked, highly attractive trails ascend to dozens of well-placed summits scattered all over the island. Shore rambles and strolls through small villages provide pleasant walking, too. The natural beauty of Mount Desert defies easy description; to say that it has few equals anywhere in America isn't hyperbole. The trail descriptions in this section provide a thorough introduction to the best of Mount Desert Island, but you'll have to see for yourself.

The lands of Acadia National Park are at the core of Mount Desert's natural attractiveness. The park is a sort of enclave within the larger boundaries of the island and contains all of the walks in this section. Some of the trails are reached only by the park service road, which may be entered at Hulls Cove

THE SHORE AT NORTHEAST HARBOR

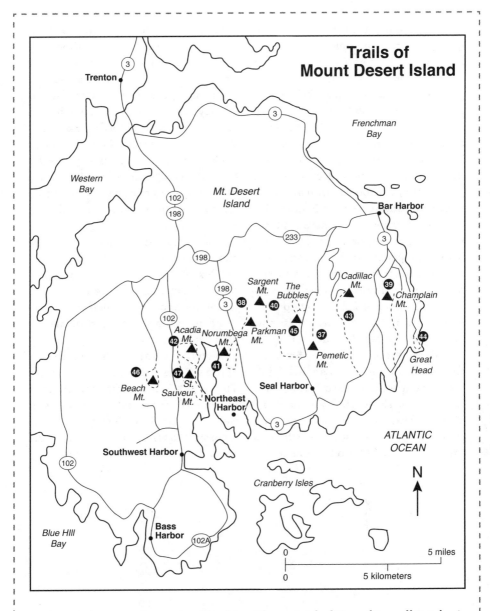

Trails of Mount Desert Island

Trenton

3

3

Frenchman Bay

Western Bay

102
198

Mt. Desert Island

Bar Harbor

233

3

198

198

3

Sargent Mt.

38

40

The Bubbles

Cadillac Mt.

39

Champlain Mt.

43

102

Acadia Mt.

42

Norumbega Mt.

Parkman Mt.

45

37

44

46

47

41

Beach Mt.

St. Sauveur Mt.

Northeast Harbor

Pemetic Mt.

Seal Harbor

Great Head

Southwest Harbor

3

ATLANTIC OCEAN

N

Cranberry Isles

Blue Hill Bay

Bass Harbor

102A

0   5 miles
0   5 kilometers

in the north or at other points on the island. An entrance fee must be paid to use this road and other park facilities. Other hikes on the island are reached on toll-free state roads (see each hike description for access directions). Acadia also features campgrounds, picnic areas, boat-launch ramps, and beaches. A complete guide to park facilities may be found at the Hulls Cove entrance.

The revised edition of Russell Butcher's *Field Guide to Acadia National Park, Maine* (Taylor Trade Publishing), available in local stores, is must reading.

The best time to visit Mount Desert is during the months of October through May. High summer tends to be crowded, and the island's narrow roads fill up with that quintessential American phenomenon, the motorized sightseer. You won't see this person on the trails, for he never gets far from an automobile. He does, however, make it harder to get to that trailhead you're in search of. If you visit Acadia in the off-season, you'll find nary a person in the woods and that serene beauty for which Acadia is famous won't be overrun with motorbound visitors. There are plenty of accommodations in the Ellsworth–Mount Desert region. Indeed, they are too plentiful and draw more congestion each year. Park service officials are urging local merchants not to overbuild, but, rather, to accommodate more people in the off-seasons. I concur with this advice, and you can do your part in preventing overuse by visiting from after Labor Day up until Memorial Day. Park-operated buses now cruise park lands in the summer.

Mount Desert and Acadia offer some fine terrain for the winter snowshoer or cross-country skier. The carriage roads are ideal for ski touring, and portions of most of the walks in this section can be snowshoed in-season. The summits are often icy and blown free of snow in winter, so good boots and instep crampons (available at most mountaineering stores) are advisable. Don't let winter drive you away, though; it's a spectacularly pretty time of year on the island.

Bicyclists will enjoy Acadia, too, as many of the carriage roads make excellent bike routes, and the loop around Eagle Lake has been specially graded for cycling. The 43 miles of carriage roads are not open to motorized vehicles, so the cyclist can enjoy the tranquility he or she craves.

For further information, write to the superintendent, Acadia National Park, PO Box 177, Bar Harbor, ME 04609. Call 207-288-3338, or visit the park's Web site at www.nps.gov/acad. If you plan to camp in Acadia, contact park officials in advance for reservations.

Note: Several hikes require an approach via the Park Service road. This is a toll road with fees charged to support year-round maintenance. A weeklong pass is available that makes it possible to visit on multiple days (and multiple hikes) at reasonable cost.

37

Pemetic Mountain

DISTANCE (ROUND TRIP): 2.5 miles

HIKING TIME: 2 hours

VERTICAL RISE: 950 feet

MAPS: USGS 15' Acadia National Park and Vicinity; AMC map of Mount Desert Island

Rising nearly in the center of Mount Desert's "eastern half," Pemetic Mountain provides some excellent views east toward Cadillac and west to Sargent Mountain, and to the parklands to the north on Eagle Lake. A bit out of the way and less frequented than some other climbs on the island, Pemetic offers you exceptional rewards as a first, short hike.

The Pemetic Mountain Trail, which runs the full length of the ridge and terminates at ME 3 in Seal Harbor, begins at the north end of Bubble Pond. To reach Bubble Pond, go south on the park service road, which leaves ME 3 at park headquarters above Hulls Cove (northwest of Bar Harbor). Park your car in the area provided at the north shore of the pond (off the park service road). *Note:* The Park Service road is a toll road.

The name Pemetic derives from local Native American parlance, meaning simply "a range of hills." From the north end of the pond, you head southwest, traveling along the west shore briefly, passing through cedar groves, then turning due west and crossing over one of the many carriage roads that traverse the island.

Past the road, you swing southwest again, walking easily through a second cedar grove at 0.3 miles. Passing through a range of some fine, tall firs, you begin to climb more steadily, moving south-southwesterly toward the summit. This area is densely grown with evergreens and provides some truly pleasant walking. It's a movie-set kind of forest. At 0.6 miles, the trail runs more southerly, passing a boulder-strewn way and along the ledges on the east side of the mountain. There is a good view of Cadillac Mountain to your left as you walk this section.

Turning more westerly, the trail soon

LOOKING NORTH THROUGH MORNING MIST TOWARD EAGLE LAKE

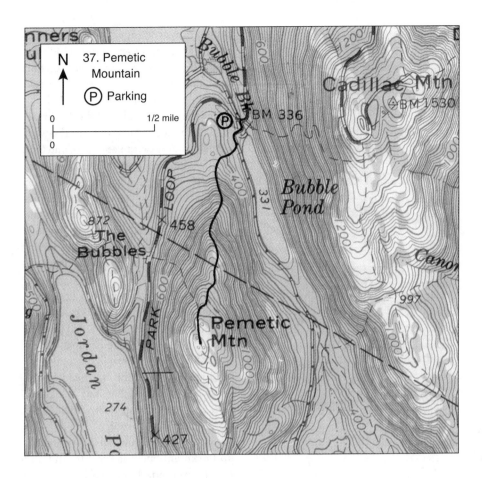

brings you to a second ledgy area, where outlooks to the north appear. On clear days, when weather isn't "making" in the valleys, good views of Eagle Lake are yours here. Continuing in the same direction, the second, more open, summit will be reached in about 650 feet.

From the summit, the striking, bare ridge to the west is Penobscot and Sargent Mountains. Almost due north of the Pemetic summit, you can see the full length of Eagle Lake, while to the east and northeast is the long rise of Cadillac Mountain. The open ledges on which you're standing are extensive and make for interesting exploring. There are several good spots on the ledges to rest and have lunch before heading down.

In descending to Bubble Pond on your return, watch the trail carefully. The dense growth makes it easy to take a wrong turn as you head down. Cairns and red blazes help mark the trail. A general northeast course cannot fail to bring you to the road should you lose the trail.

38

Parkman Mountain and Bald Peak

DISTANCE (ROUND TRIP): 2.5 miles
HIKING TIME: 2 hours
VERTICAL RISE: 700 feet
MAPS: USGS 15′ Acadia National Park and Vicinity; AMC map of Mount Desert Island

On a sunny, summer day at the height of the season, when many of Mount Desert's trails may have more hikers on them than you care to contend with, two low summits northeast of the Hadlock ponds make an excellent hike. Parkman Mountain and Bald Peak form the west leg of a triangle with Penobscot and Sargent Mountains and furnish fine vantage points over lands to the north and west of the island. These two mountains are really no more than hills, but the easy hike into both provides pleasant walking over varied terrain, and you're likely to have the summits pretty much to yourself.

To reach the trailhead, drive west from Bar Harbor on ME 233 or east from Somesville on ME 198. At the junction of the two roads, continue south on ME 198 for about 3 miles, watching for the parking lot by the trailhead on the east side of the road. You may also reach this spot by driving north on ME 198 from Northeast Harbor.

A rough trail runs almost directly up Parkman, but it is hard to find and poorly marked. A more reliable route begins at the northeast corner of the parking area on a short link to a carriage road. Take this link and turn right, walking uphill to the southeast, arriving in minutes at a junction. Bear sharply *left* at the junction, continuing upward on another unpaved road through a long S-curve. At the top of the curve, about 0.25 miles above, watch for trail signs on your left.

Turn off the road at the trail signs and walk northwest over a ledgy shelf through groves of pitch pines. The trail recrosses the road at the top of the rise and, turning more northward, enters the woods again. Your route here lies over more sandy ledge amid thin, mixed growth and curves gradually around to

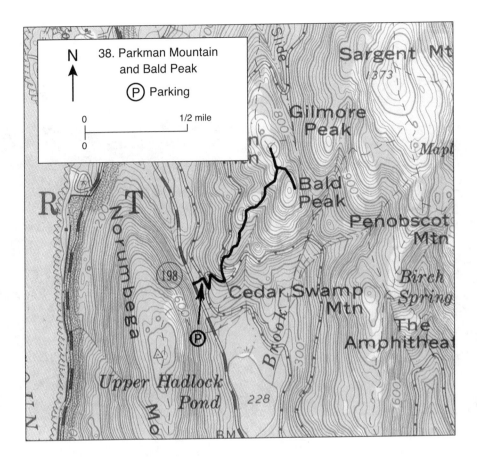

the east. The trail shortly passes through a grove of cedars, and levels off briefly, running east-northeast. Early views of Bald Peak's summit may be had here. The trail is marked with small cairns and paint blazes.

Approximately 0.6 miles from the parking area, a more pronounced scramble up the rocks begins, with occasional views to the north opening up. You drop briefly into a depression and then climb briskly eastward on a series of bare ledges. Excellent views of both Upper and Lower Hadlock Ponds emerge in this section. In minutes, you slab east-northeast over a knob and above a shallow ravine to your right. The ridge, with Parkman Mountain to your left and Bald Peak to your right, lies just above

with fine outlooks to the northwest and west as you ascend.

At the top of the ridge, a link trail runs south-southeast to Bald Peak. Turn right here, dropping into a wooded cleft between the two summits. The link rises quickly, and in 0.25 miles you crest the granite summit of aptly named Bald Peak. Excellent views of the Hadlock ponds and the lowlands, down the valley to Northeast Harbor, are to the south here. Greening Island and the open Atlantic lie to the south-southwest. Immediately to the west over the arm of land you have just climbed, you will see the north-south expanse of Norumbega Mountain (see Hike 41). Penobscot and Cedar Swamp Mountains are to the east and southeast.

PARKMAN AND BALD MOUNTAINS OVER UPPER HADLOCK POND

To reach Parkman Mountain, retrace your steps to the ridgetop trail junction, then turn right (northward) on the trail over the ledges. You'll arrive on Parkman's 940-foot summit in moments. From this totally bare mound of rock, you have a superb vantage point over the northern reaches of Somes Sound and, beyond Somesville, Western Bay. On clear days, you can also see Blue Hill, Bald Mountain, and Mount Waldo on the mainland to the west. The low summit of Acadia Mountain is visible over the northern flanks of Norumbega Mountain to the immediate west. Sargent and Penobscot Mountains make up the bright stone ridge across the ravine to the east.

Although Parkman and Bald are not high by the standard of many other mountains in Maine, they still can be very windy. Winds from the south seem to accelerate as they come up the valley from the ocean, and may often reach gale velocity on days when it's warm and calm at roadside.

To regain the road, head down on the Parkman Mountain Trail by which you ascended, using caution not to lose the trail where it crosses the carriage road.

Gorham and Champlain Mountains

DISTANCE (ROUND TRIP): 6 miles

HIKING TIME: 4 hours

VERTICAL RISE: 1,200 feet

MAPS: USGS 7.5′ Seal Harbor, ME; USGS 15′ Acadia National Park and Vicinity; AMC map of Mount Desert Island

Together, Gorham and Champlain Mountains form the easternmost north-south ridge on Mount Desert Island. Because their summits look down on a splendid coastline, the ridge walk is one of the best on the island. The hike here is over both peaks, from south to north, and returning.

Leave your car at the Monument Cove parking lot (indicated by a Gorham Mountain trail sign) on Ocean Drive about 1 mile south of Sand Beach and 1 mile north of Otter Cliffs. Take the Gorham Mountain Trail, which starts on the west side of the road, opposite the cove. Watch for the marker. Climb easily over open ledges for about 0.3 miles, passing the Cadillac Cliffs Loop Trail on your right. (You may take a detour for the cliffs; the loop rejoins the main trail about a 0.3 miles higher up.)

Your walk above the cliffs continues, rising very slightly over open ledges with good views, passes the other end of the Cliffs Loop at about 0.6 miles, and proceeds north to the open summit at just under 1 mile. There are superb north-to-south views of the island's southeast coast here.

Over the summit, descend for 0.3 miles to a connection with the Champlain Mountain Trail. Turn northwest (left) at this junction. You ascend the south ridge of Champlain gradually, proceeding around the Bowl (a mountain tarn), which is on your right, then turn north on the open ridge with more excellent views of the ocean to the east. The summit of Champlain is reached after slightly less than 3 miles of hiking from the trailhead.

From the summit, you'll see Huguenot Head tumble northwest toward Dorr and Cadillac Mountains. The community of Bar Harbor is north-northeast from your vantage point, and Bar, Sheep

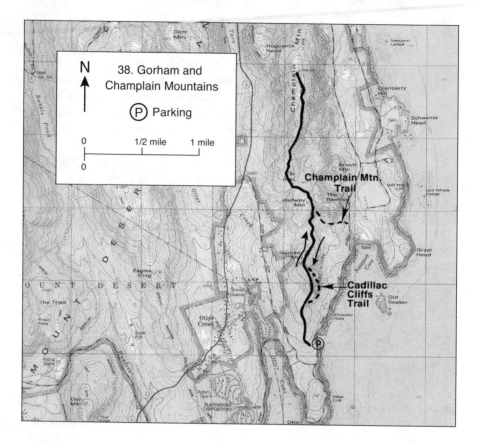

38. Gorham and Champlain Mountains

P Parking

0   1/2 mile   1 mile

0

Champlain Mtn. Trail

Cadillac Cliffs Trail

Porcupine, Burnt Porcupine, and Long Porcupine Islands stand off the harbor. You will see a point of land to the southeast, above Newport Cove, which is Great Head. The long stretch of water above Bar Harbor is Frenchman Bay.

Located on this great bay, Mount Desert Island has played an intimate role in Maine's coastal history. There are signs of habitation on the island prior to 4,000 B.C. The island was a favorite summer home of the Passamaquoddy and Penobscot tribes of the Abenaki nation prior to the colonial period. The Native

Americans wintered at their tribal homes near Orono, Maine, paddling to the island and other coastal destinations in birchbark canoes in the warm months to fish and gather provisions.

To return via your ascent route, simply turn around on the Champlain summit and head back along the ridge and then down to where you parked.

Note: Some trail restrictions have been in effect here in recent years to protect nesting peregrine falcons. Check with park headquarters to determine if restrictions are in place.

THE CLIFFS OF CHAMPLAIN MOUNTAIN

Penobscot and Sargent Mountains

DISTANCE (ROUND TRIP): 5 miles

HIKING TIME: 3 hours, 30 minutes

VERTICAL RISE: 1,150 feet

MAPS: USGS 15' Acadia National Park and Vicinity; AMC map of Mount Desert Island

Penobscot and Sargent Mountains form the high ridge that runs down to the west side of Jordan Pond. Leave your car at the new Jordan Pond House, a popular eating place just north of Seal Harbor on the park service road. The trail begins from the rear of the house. Watch for an arrow, indicating the trail to the west.

After a short walk from the house, cross the carriage road and bear slightly to your right over a footbridge spanning Jordan Stream. Follow signs for the Penobscot Mountain Trail. You travel west and northwest, rising very gradually for the first 0.3 miles. The trail then climbs more rapidly for a while, levels off briefly, descends to cross another brook, and turns left below a wall of granite boulders.

Slabbing left up the wall, cross a second carriage road and resume the steep northwesterly pitch up the ridge. The climb becomes very interesting here, and you will traverse several rock ledges that are nearly perpendicular. *Caution is required.* Be very careful not to dislodge loose rock, which could fall on a climber below. The trail here follows a series of switchbacks, with some straight vertical climbing.

After maneuvering up through a narrow crack and around another switchback, you emerge onto a ledge (right) with excellent views down to Jordan Pond and across the water to Pemetic Mountain. The two round peaks known as the Bubbles are to your left at the far end of the pond. Continue west now, climbing through a wooded area to an open ledge at the peak of the south ridge. Turn abruptly right here and head north along the ridge toward the Penobscot summit.

The views are very good on the

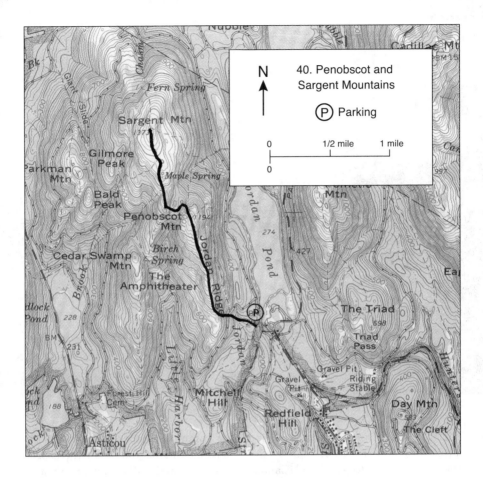

ridge (you can see almost full circle, from northeast to northwest) and get progressively better as you near the top. The trail meanders over the bare ridge, passing several false summits, and reaches the true summit, directly opposite Pemetic, at 1.5 miles.

The summit of Sargent Mountain is just under 1 mile north. Below you to the northwest is Sargent Pond, a tiny alpine lake. To reach the pond, take the Sargent Pond Trail from the summit of Penobscot. The descent to the pond is quickly made over ledgy terrain. The South Ridge Trail is well marked and leads from the pond directly to the top of Sargent, 0.75 miles farther. Allow at

least an additional half hour to get over to Sargent.

Looking south from either peak, you will quickly come to appreciate why climbing on Mount Desert Island is unique. Besides the excellent mountain views to the west, north, and east, there are superb views of the Atlantic to the south. The point of land to the southeast is Seal Harbor, and out beyond are the islands that lie off Mount Desert's southern shores. The largest, slightly to the left, is Great Cranberry Island. To the northeast lie Little Cranberry and Baker Islands. The three smaller islands closer to the shore are, left to right, Sutton, Bear, and Greening. Farther out,

PENOBSCOT MOUNTAIN OVER LONG POND

Little Duck and Great Duck may be visible if the weather is exceptionally clear. Having surveyed the peaks and islands, head down to the Jordan Pond House via the long, splendid walk south on the Penobscot Trail.

Although Penobscot and Sargent are low summits compared with Maine's major mountains, you should travel prepared. As on Cadillac and Champlain, these ridges are open to harsh wind and weather and offer little shelter. Be sure to carry extra clothing in case of sudden changes in the weather.

Norumbega Mountain Loop

DISTANCE (AROUND LOOP): 2.75 miles	
HIKING TIME: 2 hours	
VERTICAL RISE: 600 feet	
MAPS: USGS 15′ Acadia National Park and Vicinity; AMC map of Mount Desert Island	

Physically, Mount Desert Island is a heart-shaped land mass, divided in the middle by fjordlike Somes Sound, and peppered with bare summits rising dramatically from the sea. Norumbega Mountain is a low summit that forms the eastern wall of the sound and provides nearly as much good hiking as many of its higher neighbors on the mainland. The views, as one would expect, are first-class.

On its eastern perimeter, Norumbega lies side by side with Upper and Lower Hadlock Ponds. The summit, besides monitoring the length of the sound, looks south to the lowlands of Southwest Harbor and Tremont. Norumbega also forms the left leg of a horseshoe-shaped series of peaks whose eastern border consists of Sargent and Penobscot Mountains. The mountain was formerly known as Brown's Mountain after John Brown, an early settler who owned a major plot of land north of the rise.

To reach the mountain from the junction of ME 198 and ME 233, take ME 198 south along the eastern edge of Somes Sound. At 2.8 miles from the junction, watch for a parking area on the west side of the road, just above Upper Hadlock Pond.

From the parking area, walk westward on the Norumbega Mountain Trail. Ascending steeply, you turn northwestward—away from the summit—slab the ridge, and then turn south at about 0.3 miles. The climb continues southward, rising over more open granite ledges (with scattered views) and reaches the summit at about 0.6 miles. The summit is wooded, but allows fine, open views to the west and up the sound. The mountains across the water are Saint Sauveur and Acadia. Farther back are Bernard, Mansell, and Beach

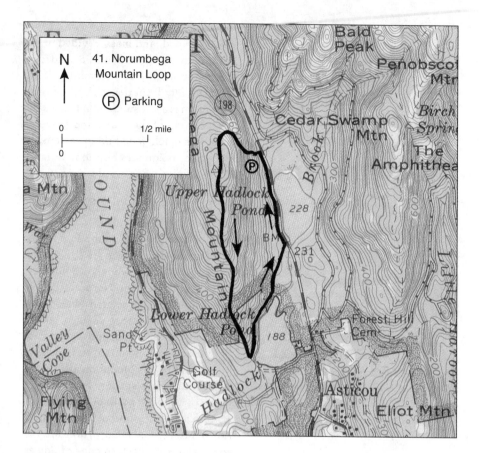

Mountains, ranging left to right, one almost behind the other. Rest a while here and soak it all up.

There are blueberry bushes on the north ridge, and if you climb in midsummer you can gather the makings of a pie before leaving the summit. Underway again, continue down the trail to the south. The walk through mixed fir, pine, and spruce straddles the south ridge. The trail descends easily offering fine views and, about 1.6 miles from the parking lot, reaches the west shore of Lower Hadlock Pond. You turn sharply northeast here, following the *west* shore of the pond. *Keeping west* of the pond and its northern brook, you reach Route 198 at 2.25 miles. Turn left (north) on the road that takes you back to your starting point, not quite 0.75 miles away.

A HIKING PATH ON MOUNT DESERT ISLAND

42

Acadia Mountain Loop

DISTANCE (AROUND LOOP): 2.5 miles

HIKING TIME: 1 hour, 30 minutes

VERTICAL RISE: 500 feet

MAPS: USGS 7.5′ Southwest Harbor, ME;
USGS 15′ Acadia National Park and Vicinity;
AMC map of Mount Desert Island

Acadia Mountain is one of the attractive, low summits that border Somes Sound on the western half of Mount Desert Island. The sound, which many consider the only real coastal fjord in eastern America (because the mountains plunge right down to the sea here), rolls south to the sea directly under Acadia's east peak. You'll be able to approach the sound on the lower reaches of this hike where the trail crosses Man of War Brook. The area, a supremely attractive hiking ground, has many historic associations. Nearby Saint Sauveur Mountain bears the name of the early French colony on the island, founded in 1613. The colony was destroyed in a matter of weeks by marauding English coastal patrols. The English men-of-war found the deep waters of the sound a good place to drop anchor close to shore. Fresh water from Man of War Brook and fish and game from the area replenished the larders of the English fighting ships.

The west-to-east traverse of Acadia Mountain begins on ME 102, 3 miles south of Somesville and 3 miles north of Southwest Harbor. A large parking area on the west side of the road above Echo Lake is situated opposite the trailhead. The trail runs east over a bluff and into the woods. Quickly ascending a series of ledges, you walk east-southeast through groves of pitch pines and birches, which are surrounded by blueberry bushes.

You shortly reach a junction, and turn north (left) through a slump overgrown with rhodora, thence climbing slightly over several ledgy ribs. In moments you cross gravel Robinson Road, reenter the woods, and directly ascend a low ledge. The trail now rises more steeply north-northeastward to a second ledgy area, where views to the west begin to open up. You curve

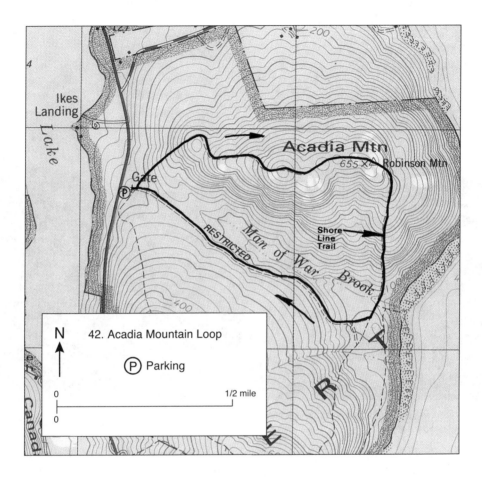

Ikes Landing

Lake

Acadia Mtn

655 X Robinson Mtn

Gate

RESTRICTED

Man of War Brook

Shore Line Trail

N

42. Acadia Mountain Loop

ⓟ Parking

| 0 | | 1/2 mile |

0

Cadad

400

around to the east-southeast over the attractive exposed granite, passing through a shady depression filled with thickly grown pine and Indian pipes. Early views of the south end of the sound may be seen here. In a few more minutes you reach Acadia's west summit, which has spectacular views to the south but is wooded on its north side. (A short side trail leads to a bald spot with good views on the north lip of the knob.) Although you'll be pleased with what you see from this spot, there are even better views from the east peak. To get there, simply walk eastward through a depression grown up with stunted oak and rho-

dora, emerging on the east summit in a few minutes.

Acadia's east knob provides a splendid outlook on Somes Sound and the offshore islands to the south. Beautiful Valley Cove is below to the near south, and above it to the right lies Saint Sauveur Mountain. Flying Mountain is the low hill that juts into the water beyond the cove. Across the water, the hulk of Norumbega Mountain runs north and south. The peak to the west with the prominent tower is Beech Mountain. A number of large sailing craft are usually moored around the cove in fair weather. The prospect from this side of Acadia is profoundly beautiful, and you'll want

ACADIA MOUNTAIN (RIGHT) AND NORUMBEGA MOUNTAIN OVER SOMES SOUND

to allow time to sit on the rocks here, enjoying it all.

To descend to Man of War Brook, head east of the summit over rolling ledges and down into groves of red oak. The trail turns south and makes its way over several ledges in switchbacks that are moderately steep. At 0.5 miles below the east peak, you enter a cedar grove and cross the brook. A link trail to your left leads 100 yards to the shoreline. Continue south on the main trail, turning southwest (right) at a trail junction.

You next cross a field and reach the end of Robinson Road. Follow the road northwest as it rises gently, passing very attractive groves of cedar. There are periodic views of the bare ledges of Acadia's west peak before you enter the woods here.

Continue along the road to the northwest for about 0.5 miles, watching for trail signs at the crossing. Turn left (west) at the point where you crossed the road originally, and retrace your steps to ME 102 in another 0.25 miles.

43

Cadillac Mountain

DISTANCE (ROUND TRIP): 7 miles	
HIKING TIME: 4 hours, 30 minutes	
VERTICAL RISE: 1,230 feet	
MAPS: USGS 15' Acadia National Park and Vicinity; AMC map of Mount Desert Island	

Cadillac Mountain, Mount Desert's highest summit, broods over the eastern half of the island, its great 5-mile-long bulk visible from almost anywhere on the land or water around it. The mountain, named after Antoine Cadillac, who was given the island by Louis XIV in 1688, offers what is perhaps the best extended walk along open heights on the island. The walk culminates in superb views over the entire island, Frenchman Bay, and the Atlantic.

To ascend Cadillac, drive south from Bar Harbor on Route 3. Watch for trail signs on the north side of the road nearly opposite the entrance to Black Woods Campground. There is ample room to park cars on the shoulder of the road. From the road, the trail immediately enters thick woods, running north and northwest on a gradual rise through close-grown balsam, white pine, and cedar. The ground cover has been eroded in many places, and the distinctive pink granite of the island frequently protrudes.

Walk through scattered boulders and rock slabs, arriving at a junction with the loop to Eagle Crag on your right in 1 mile. Eagle Crag offers much the same views as the main trail. Keep left here and stay on the main trail under the rock outcrops, climbing northwestward to the first open ledges, with views to the southwest. At just over 1.5 miles from the road, the trail wanders through birch and groves of jack pine into open, 180-degree views to the south. On summer days, a great deal of sailing activity around the islands to the south can be seen from here.

The trail continues over open ledges and through occasional scrub along the north-south rib of the mountain. Interesting dikes of metamorphosed shale are seen here and there in the rock, and the summit appears ahead to your right.

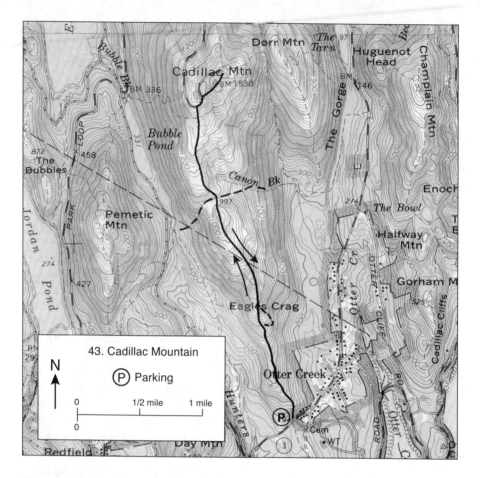

43. Cadillac Mountain

Ⓟ Parking

N

0   1/2 mile   1 mile

0

You may also look east, taking in the whole range of Gorham and Champlain Mountains, including the tiny mountain tarn known as the Bowl. About 1 mile below the summit, the route descends into a gully, passing a weedy bog to your left and crossing the Canon Brook Trail.

For the remainder of the route below the summit, you walk completely in the open, and all vegetation ceases. Winds in this area can be uncomfortable in rough weather. Continuing north-northeast across the open slab, the trail loops to the edge of the road, then runs through a wooded area to the summit over short, easy grades. In a few minutes, you pass the true summit to your left behind

the service building and emerge at the summit parking area. The open ledges with the best views lie a short walk to the east.

Cadillac's summit, being the highest on the island, offers fine views in all directions. You'll see Dorr Mountain rising in the immediate foreground to the east. Behind it, the long ridge of Champlain Mountain, named after the island's discoverer, stands between Dorr and the sea. The islands in Bar Harbor and Frenchman Bay are to the northeast. Schoodic Point, also a part of Acadia National Park, lies far across the bay to the east. Pemetic, Penobscot, and Sargent Mountains constitute the

CADILLAC MOUNTAIN FROM SOMESVILLE

most imposing summits to the west, and are best seen in their entirety from the summit's west parking area.

From up here, it isn't hard to see why Mount Desert became such a hotly contested prize among the early colonial settlers. Discovered and first colonized by the French, the island later passed into British hands before being taken by the American colonials. Its abundant excellent harbors, game, and notable water supplies made it a treasure worth pursuing as a base for controlling the surrounding waters.

To return to your car at Black Woods, retrace your route downward. The walk from the 1,500-foot summit to ME 3 can be done in less than two hours.

44

Sand Beach and Great Head

DISTANCE (ROUND TRIP): 2 miles

HIKING TIME: 1 hour, 30 minutes

VERTICAL RISE: 200 feet

MAPS: USGS 7.5′ Seal Harbor, ME; USGS 15′ Acadia National Park and Vicinity; AMC map of Mount Desert Island

One of the most attractive stretches of shoreline on Mount Desert Island, Sand Beach and Great Head provide the walker with an easy route through varied, always beautiful terrain. The Head itself gives the hiker access to what are probably the best shoreline views on the east side of the island across the water to the Schoodic Peninsula. And since the elevation gains on this route are minor, it's a good walk with youngsters or an undemanding stroll on a day when you'd like to mosey along the shore, avoiding the steeper climbs of Mount Desert's higher summits.

From Bar Harbor, head south on ME 3, reaching a fork in the road about 1 mile from the center of town. Keep to the left here on Schooner Head Road. Stay on this road for about 3 miles, making no turns, until it terminates at a barrier. Turn around here and park in the new parking lot at the trailhead, which is marked by a wooden pillar about 200 yards before the road ends.

This walk makes a loop past Sand Beach and offers a shorter return over the inland ledges of the head, or a longer walk along the perimeter of the head, rejoining the shorter loop on the return. Both walks are undemanding and, except for a brief scramble up the ledges, require little climbing.

Begin by walking south on the trail through white birch, steeplebush, and spruce. The route lies over a broad woods road now turned grassy and well shaded. In a few hundred feet, you will pass the return leg of the path coming in on your left. Proceed straight ahead, and reach the bluffs over Sand Beach in 0.5 miles. Spectacular views over the beach and up to the Beehive, a rounded granitic mountain, open up to the west. You may wish to descend to the beach

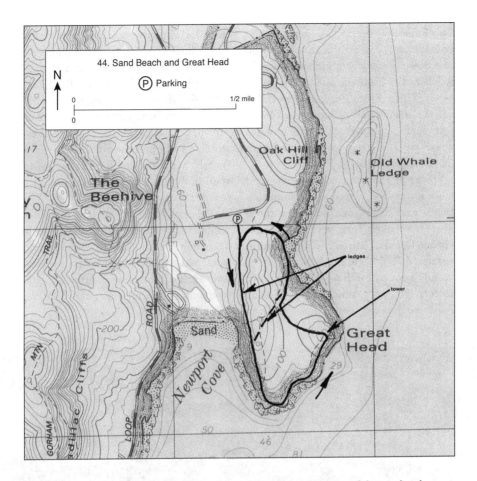

via a pathway now and explore the shore and the pretty freshwater lagoon behind it. Herons, ducks, and other shorebirds are often seen, particularly in early morning. The beach itself is a fine expanse of yellow sand that caps Newport Cove. Visit here in early or late season if you can. In high summer, the crowds descend.

Opposite the point where the side trail descends to the beach, the shorter of the two loops zigzags directly up a ledge marked with red blazes. If you wish to return this way, head up the ledge and arrive at a bare summit with superb views to the east and back to the west over the Beehive and Champlain Mountain. The route then descends

from the ledges and loops back on a well-marked trail to the junction mentioned earlier.

To reach Great Head, continue south and southeast, gradually rounding the end of the peninsula over mossy ground and rising and falling through aspen and birch. Following the red blazes and, later, cairns, you'll soon arrive at the ruined stone tower near Great Head's 145-foot, precipitous drop to the broad Atlantic. You can see in all directions here: back to the mountains of the island, southeast to the open ocean, to the east across Frenchman Bay to the Schoodic region, and northeast to the mountains of the mainland. The squarish building on the tiny island is

Egg Rock lighthouse, a beacon for the considerable water traffic that moves up and down the bay. Around to the southwest are the high, dark ledges forming Otter Cliffs. From here, you can also see the Beehive and Champlain Mountain again, along whose summit ridges there are excellent, long, north-south day hikes (see Hike 39).

To return, leave the tower site and walk northwest, descending soon to a boggy area over more ledge. Scattered alders, bracken fern, and occasional spruce line the path as you move within earshot of the shore. Just beyond a thick stand of young birch where the ground is carpeted with bunchberry, Canada mayflower, moss, and lichen, you join the shorter of the two loop trails as it comes in on your left. Continuing northwest over easy grades, the trail broadens and becomes less stony. Reaching a height-of-land in a small clearing, descend slightly, curving more westerly, and soon reach the main trail on which you began the walk. Bear right (north) here, and you'll gain the paved road and your parking place in just a few minutes.

This walk can also be done in milder winters when there is likely to be little snow cover on the island. Good hiking boots should always be worn in winter and during inclement weather, as the frequent ledge-walking on this hike can be slippery.

SAND BEACH

The Bubbles

DISTANCE (ROUND TRIP): 3.5 miles	
HIKING TIME: 2 hours	
VERTICAL RISE: 800 feet	
MAPS: USGS 15' Acadia National Park and Vicinity; AMC map of Mount Desert Island	

The Bubbles are two 800-foot mounds of pink granite that dominate the northern end of Jordan Pond in the east-central portion of Mount Desert Island. The sister mountains form a striking profile that at first may discourage the hiker with no technical climbing experience. In fact, these two very rocky peaks require no special mountaineering skills and are readily accessible to the average hiker. The Bubbles not only offer a challenging outing for the hiker, but they also are an elegant platform in the midst of Acadia National Park for viewing nearly all of the major summits that surround it.

This hike is directly reached by driving ME 3 east from Ellsworth to the north end of Mount Desert Island and turning onto the park service road at the Hulls Cove entrance. An information center is just inside this entrance; ask for directions and park maps here if you need them. Proceed south on the park service road to the Bubble Rock parking area north of Jordan Pond. This spot is also known as the "Bubble-Pemetic" parking area, and shouldn't be confused with the "Bubbles" parking lot still another 0.5 miles farther south.

The walk begins to the west from the parking area, rising up through closely grown beech, birch, and striped maple. You reach a junction in less than 650 feet and cross the Jordan Pond Carry Trail. From here, continue straight on up an old tote road, bearing gradually to the left, over several water bars, arriving shortly at another junction. Trails lead from this junction to both of the Bubble summits.

Bear left and ascend the trail to the South Bubble. The climb is brisk up through young beech and birch. With Pemetic Mountain off to your left, you keep left at the junction with the trail

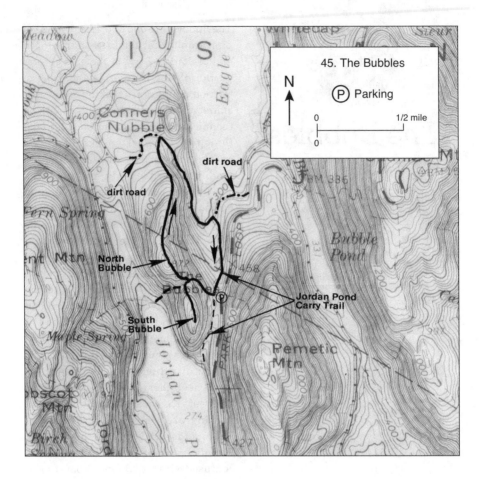

from Jordan Pond. Views to the North Bubble begin to open up behind you now. At just under 800 feet, the summit of the South Bubble is an open expanse of glacier-scarred granite, onto which you soon emerge after a final march amid scraggly birch and alder.

Potassium feldspar accounts for the characteristic pink glow of Mount Desert's coarse granite hills. The igneous stone was formed approximately 350 million years ago and has been glacially scoured several times since, most recently 18,000 to 11,000 years ago. The Laurentide ice sheet, the most recent of the glacial waves to come down from the northwest over New England, was roughly 5,000 feet thick as it built up

and then slid over this range. One effect of the ice was the pleasing, rounded shape of the mountains in this area, further aided by subsequent weathering. As the ice moved through any depressions, it ground and chiseled them until they became the valleys that run characteristically north and south on Mount Desert.

The north and northwest sides of most mountains in Acadia bear glacial scars from the grinding, rolling action of stone and sand carried along by glacial ice. As the ice moved over these ranges, the mobile sand and stone were dragged under tremendous pressure across existing formations. Those mountains' southern and southeastern sides of Mount

Desert show rather sheer, precipitous faces due to the circular motion of glacially carried rock known as "plucking." Both of the Bubbles exhibit scarring and plucking.

Jordan and Great Ponds give you a sense of how efficient glacial action could be at scraping off deposits and carrying them away. The ponds are quite deep from the scouring and transporting action of sheet ice. The material dredged from these spots by the action of the ice was deposited farther down at the south ends of the valleys. The action of the great ice sheets also transported large boulders, called glacial erratics, from distances as great as 20 miles. One of the most prominent of these erratics can be seen just a few yards south of the South Bubble summit.

When you've had a chance to look around at the surrounding hills, descend to the junction with the North Bubble Trail, turning left and beginning the walk up the second peak. The route is to the north through more dwarf birch and over ledge with Pemetic and Cadillac Mountains in striking profile to the east and northeast. You'll soon pass several cairns and proceed over the creased

NORTH BUBBLE (RIGHT) AND PEMETIC MOUNTAIN OVER EAGLE LAKE

granite mentioned earlier. Mountain cranberries lie beneath a corridor of young pitch pines and red spruces as you walk on the summit of North Bubble.

From this second peak, a beautiful view of Eagle Lake to the north greets you. Beyond it, farther to the northeast is the great expanse of Frenchman Bay. Off to the west is the long massif of Penobscot and Sargent Mountains. This more northerly of the two Bubbles is the higher, at nearly 900 feet, and from it you can look back over the route you've followed thus far, and also ahead to the route down to the north along the ridge toward Conners Nubble and Eagle Lake.

Head down the open ridge, which supports little growth, having been burned over in the great Bar Harbor fires of 1947. Follow the cairns down the ledges, enjoying the continuing views of Cadillac, Acadia's highest mountain, as you proceed northward. A little more than 0.75 mile below the north summit, you reach a carriage trail. Bear right and east here and walk another 0.75 miles downhill into the woods until you reach the Jordan Pond Carry Trail. Turn right here onto this sometimes wet, boggy trail and ascend slowly through beech and hemlock groves to the first trail junction of this hike. At the junction, go left and you'll regain the parking area in a couple of minutes.

Beech Mountain

DISTANCE (AROUND LOOP): 3.5 miles

HIKING TIME: 2 hours, 30 minutes

VERTICAL RISE: 700 feet

MAPS: USGS 7.5′ Southwest Harbor, ME;
USGS 15′ Acadia National Park and Vicinity;
AMC map of Mount Desert Island

Beech Mountain, one of a circle of low hills in the remote western quarter of Mount Desert Island, is notable for its unspoiled beauty. Situated on the little-traveled west side of Echo Lake, Beech Mountain is the highest point on a long ridge separating Echo Lake and the much larger Long Pond. A variety of paths winds around the mountain through attractive woods, boulder gardens, and splendid, open ledges. Except for the initial gain in altitude, the trail is not difficult or demanding. Even a beginning hiker will find this an easy and very pleasant walk.

To reach the mountain, follow ME 3 south and east from Ellsworth to its junction with ME 102 and ME 198 just beyond the Thompson Island Information Center as you enter Mount Desert Island. Bear right and follow ME 102 to Somesville. From the center of this little village, bear right 0.3 miles past Higgins Market and continue on ME 102 as it heads west. In less than 0.25 miles, you bear left onto Beech Hill Road. The road runs south along a high ridge, gradually leaves the houses behind, and rolls toward Beech Mountain. Pretty, open fields, grown thick with low-bush blueberries, yield fine views to Beech and to Bernard and Mansell Mountains to the southwest and to other ranges on the island off to the east.

Beech Hill Road ends abruptly at a parking lot just over 3 miles from its junction with ME 102. Park to the right under the cliffs. Take the trail that leaves the northwest corner of the parking area. This trail moves upward to the west for several hundred yards before coming to a trail junction. Keep to the left at the junction and take the higher of two trails to the summit. On this route, you shortly move onto open ledge with excellent outlooks back to

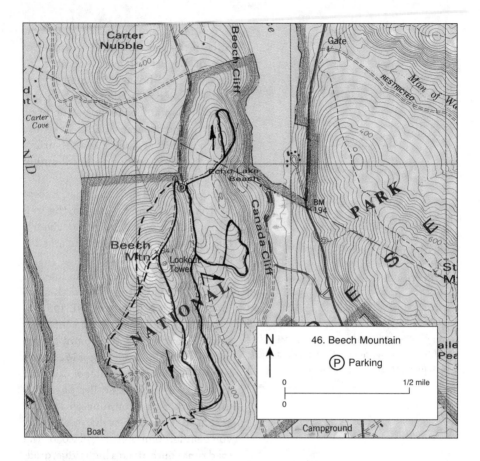

the north over Echo Lake and to Somesville, with its prominent white church steeple. Good views across Somes Sound to Norumbega and Penobscot Mountains are found here. In less than 0.5 mile from the parking lot, you arrive at the convergence of the two trails at the observation tower on Beech's 839-foot summit.

Beech's summit plateau, overgrown with sheep laurel, provides 360-degree views including those to the south toward Greening Island, the Cranberry Isles, and the Atlantic. Mansell and Bernard Mountains loom to the southwest across the southern neck of Long Pond. The pond, a beautiful, slim expanse of water running north and south, is the largest landlocked body of water on Mount Desert.

To continue beyond the summit, take the South Ridge Trail toward the ocean, descending a granite ridge dotted with lichen. The route is alternately in the open and in the woods. You are as likely as not to see deer tracks along here. British soldiers—tiny, red-capped lichens—cranberries, gray-green reindeer lichen, and heather grow among the rocks. Reaching a set of stone steps, take a sharp left downhill. The open ledges now give way to shady bowers of spruce. A series of switchbacks descends through mossy cascades and thick groves of birch and beech, bringing you to a junction with a side trail that runs to Long Pond. Instead, bear left onto the Valley Trail, heading away from the pond. Walk due north on the Valley Trail, passing through varied growth and past a jumble of granite slabs stacked here long ago by glacial movement. This ancient stonework is now covered with polypody fern and a foliose lichen known as rock tripe.

From where you made the turn onto the Valley Trail to the parking area is just under 1 mile. Approximately 0.6 miles along this path, you come to the Canada Cliffs Loop Trail on your right. Turn right (east) here at the sign, cross a boggy area, climb a brief rise, and then walk down through a cedar bog on a series of plank bridges. This trail shortly forks, each side being the "leg" of a loop over the cliffs. Keep right and you'll soon be on the ledges with fine views east to Saint Sauveur Mountain. The other leg of the trail comes in about 50 yards from the summit. Make a mental note of this spot, as you'll return on the other leg on your way back to the Valley Trail. A walk of a few more yards brings you to the high point on these dramatic, open cliffs with excellent outlooks to Echo Lake and the northeast. Picking up the other leg of the loop, proceed briefly west to the Valley Trail, and then turn northward (right) toward your starting place.

THE HILLS OF MOUNT DESERT OVERLOOKING SOUTHWEST HARBOR

If, when you reach the parking lot, you've got some energy left, another short loop runs off to the northeast over Beech Cliff. Look for the sign that indicates this loop across the road opposite the northeast corner of the parking lot. Keep left just past the sign and make the short walk (about 0.3 miles) through groves of spruce and cedar eastward to Beech Cliff over Echo Lake. The views over Echo Lake are even better than those you experienced on Canada Cliffs. The granite here bears the familiar scouring of glacial activity so common on the summits of Mount Desert.

After passing over the top point of this cliff, bear around to the south on a lower trail, gradually pulling west and rejoining the short leg to the parking lot. On this lower, return loop, you come around again to the fork where you stayed left on the way in. A third trail here makes a rise over a hill and then descends gradually through a series of ladders and switchbacks to Echo Lake. The walk down this trail to the water is about a 0.75-mile round trip. (The trail to the water isn't included in the time and distance estimates at the top of this hike description.)

Saint Sauveur– Flying Mountain Loop

DISTANCE (ROUND TRIP): 6 miles

HIKING TIME: 3 hours

VERTICAL RISE: 1,100 feet

MAPS: USGS 7.5′ Southwest Harbor, ME; USGS 15′ Acadia National Park and Vicinity; AMC map of Mount Desert Island

For fine views over the narrows at the south end of magnificent Somes Sound, the circle over Saint Sauveur and Flying Mountains near Southwest Harbor makes an excellent walk. This route takes the hiker over three low summits in the less-frequented quarter of Mount Desert Island. The walk is both prettily wooded in sections and also barren, ledgy, and open in places, providing a platform that looks seaward. And because Saint Sauveur lies in an area off the beaten tourist path, you can walk here with relative privacy even in high summer.

The hike begins at the same spot as the Acadia Mountain loop (see Hike 42) on ME 102, 3 miles south of Somesville and 3 miles north of Southwest Harbor. The parking area on ME 102 is well marked and easy to find directly across from the trailhead. There are some fine outlooks over Echo Lake, too, as you drive south from Somesville.

Enter the woods headed eastward on the Acadia Mountain Trail and follow this path for just a short distance before reaching the Saint Sauveur Trail on your right. Bear right here and begin the straightforward march to the southeast up the northwest flanks of Saint Sauveur. These are pretty woods, characterized by abundant Scotch pine, gray birch, and other young hardwoods. Crossing a seasonal brook and passing through several clearings, you rise gradually toward the summit with views of Acadia Mountain opening up behind you. One mile from your starting place, you pass the Ledge Trail on your right. Continue southeast another 0.3 miles, now out in the open, to the bare, ledgy summit of Saint Sauveur.

The mountain takes its name from the ill-fated French settlement established here by the Jesuits in 1613. The French

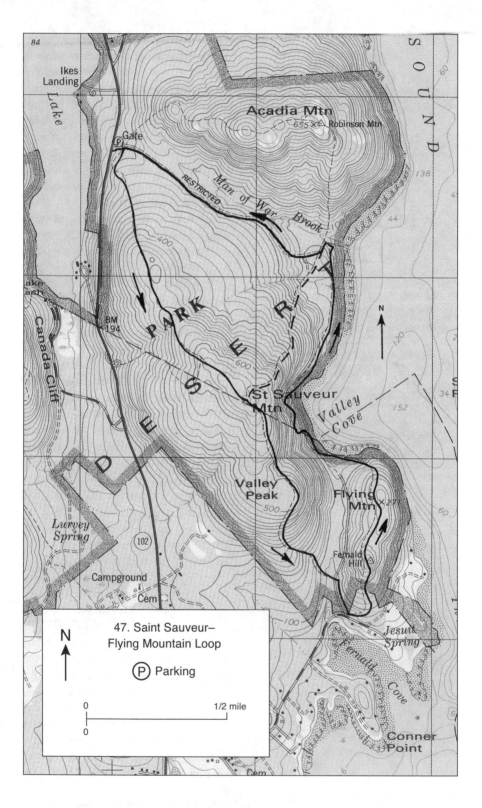

47. Saint Sauveur–Flying Mountain Loop

P Parking

N

0   1/2 mile
0

mission had set out for Bangor but was blown into Frenchman Bay by a severe storm. After exploring the south coast of the island, the missionaries decided that the lower reaches of Somes Sound seemed a good place to establish a base, particularly with fresh water available in nearby Man of War Brook. However, in just weeks the colony was discovered by the patrolling English frigate *Treasurer*, under the command of Samuel Argall.

James I of England claimed Mount Desert's shores during this period, and the mandate of English coasters was to put a stop to any French attempts to develop permanent settlements here. In full battle dress, the *Treasurer* bore down on the French ship *Jonas*, moored off Fernald Cove below Flying Moun-

tain. The French were quite unprepared for the arrival of an English 14-gunner, and fled into the woods of Saint Sauveur. Members of the short-lived colony surrendered to the British the next day. A full and colorful description of this and other military and naval actions can be found in Samuel Eliot Morison's *The Story of Mount Desert Island*, available in many shops in Bar Harbor and Ellsworth.

Saint Sauveur's summit ledges are surrounded by low spruce, so the views are less good here than on the ridge you've just come up and farther along in this hike. Proceed off the summit to Eagle Cliffs, a far better outlook, just past a clearing laced with juniper bushes. The panorama of Somes Sound,

LONG POND

spreading itself out beneath you, is magnificent, and you'll probably want to rest here a while and enjoy watching the movement of boats up and down the sound. Valley Cove is the rounded bay immediately to the east.

From Eagle Cliffs, take the left trail at a junction and descend gradually to Valley Peak through juniper and blueberry bushes. Valley Peak, an arm of Saint Sauveur Mountain, offers additional opportunities to see the ocean and the sound as you proceed southeastward. Moving through cedar and spruce cover, you walk over heavily gouged granite ledge and onto Valley Peak's 520-foot summit.

The trail next pulls around to the west, providing good views of Fernald Cove and Southwest Harbor. Gnarled oaks and white pines border the path as you descend nearly to sea level. You walk through a cedar bog and over two plank bridges, emerging in minutes on a gravel right-of-way known as Valley Cove Truck Road. Head right on the road for 100 yards, and then bear left on Flying Mountain Trail, which is clearly marked. Making the turn here, you're at the most southerly point on the walk.

The hike takes you uphill again through columns of tall cedars on Flying Mountain's south arm. Very shortly you arrive on the ledgy summit. Valley Peak, Beech, and Mansell Mountains are off to the northwest. The pot shape of Greening Island floats to the southeast off Southwest Harbor. Fernald Cove is directly below you to the south. Although Flying Mountain is the lowest of the three moderate summits in this loop, you have the feeling of being up high here because of the abrupt rise of these hills from the water.

Resuming the hike, you'll bear around to the east looking out over the narrows. If you happen to hit this spot at low tide, you'll note that Somes Sound is nearly a lake at such moments, given the shallow bar at the narrows. You now descend fairly steeply for 0.3 miles to Valley Cove. On a warm summer day, you may want to picnic here and have a swim. To get on the beach, leave the trail where it crosses a footbridge near the shore. Valley Cove Spring signs appear momentarily. This *may* be a source of water, but is unpredictable.

Skirting the cove, proceed through a collection of boulders where polypody fern, rock tripe, and moss grow. Cross a slide and ascend a series of stone steps as you move north of the cove. Eagle Cliffs hangs above you to the left on Saint Sauveur. Continuing northward, cross another slide, which requires caution, and pick up the trail again on its other side. The trail then drops to the water's edge and enters the woods.

After a short walk along the shore of the sound, enter a cedar bog and come to Man of War Brook. Watch for a woods road on your left, and turn west here. This is the same route back to the highway that one takes when completing the Acadia Mountain loop. From here, walk through a field and you'll reach the end of Robinson Road in a few hundred yards. You then continue to the northwest through groves of cedar and, staying with the trail, reach ME 102 and your car in about 0.5 miles.

VIII.

EASTERN MAINE AND THE EASTERN MAINE COAST

48

Johnson Brook Trail Circuit: Sunkhaze Meadows National Wildlife Refuge

DISTANCE: 2.5 miles

HIKING TIME: 2 hours, 30 minutes

VERTICAL RISE: About 50 feet

MAPS: USGS 7.5′ Lincoln, ME; USGS Bangor, ME; US Fish and Wildlife Service trail map available at the trailhead

Here is a hike through a 9,300-acre parcel of Maine wildlands north and east of Bangor in Milford. Free of development and now dedicated to the protection of animal and avian life, Sunkhaze Meadows National Wildlife Refuge is a US Fish and Wildlife Service–managed woodland in a national system of refuges numbering nearly 500. Bisected here and there by traces of old logging roads, Sunkhaze straddles the stream of the same name, and also smaller, feeder waters such as Little Birch Stream and Buzzy Brook.

The reserve was established in 1988 and offers a variety of terrain for walkers, including upland forest, extensive peat-capped bogland, cedar and alder swamps, and dense mixed-growth and coniferous woodland. Surrounding the second-largest of Maine peat bogs, Sunkhaze harbors ancient peat deposition 15 feet or more in thickness at some locations. The Sunkhaze Refuge also includes three smaller sites in Troy, Benton, and Unity, which offer shelter to several potentially threatened bird species.

Wildlife Service publications suggest that refuge visitors may see white-tailed deer, moose, beavers, black bears, coyotes, river otters, and fishers here. Porcupines, red squirrels, muskrats, snowshoe hares, field mice, and voles are also regularly seen. The refuge is also habitat for larger raptors, including kestrels, eastern red-tailed hawks, northern harriers, and broad-winged hawks. Barred owls and great horned owls appear consistently.

Wading birds such as great blue herons, American bitterns, rails, spotted sandpipers, and yellowlegs feed here, as do many species of waterfowl. The substantial wetlands, access to moving water, and local food sources attract birds to Sunkhaze throughout the year.

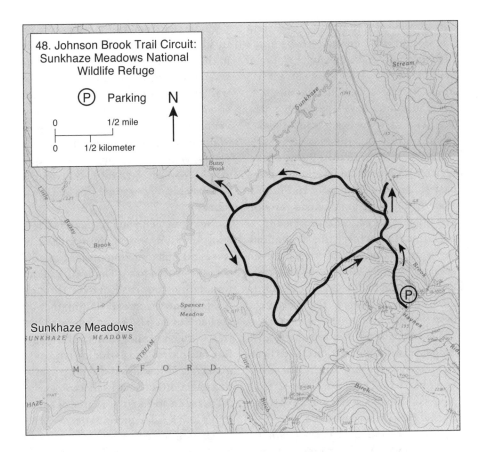

48. Johnson Brook Trail Circuit:
Sunkhaze Meadows National
Wildlife Refuge

ⓟ Parking   N

0   1/2 mile

0   1/2 kilometer

Sunkhaze Meadows

Refuge managers have recorded the presence of more than 200 species of avian wildlife within Sunkhaze.

Unlike other hiking venues noted in this book, Sunkhaze National Wildlife Refuge does not generally possess a defined and well-worn trail system. Some walks here have a certain unplanned wildness to them, all to the good. Trails out to the marshlands, Buzzy Brook, Little Buzzy Brook, and Sunkhaze Stream are typical of these less-defined routes where some compass work may be in order if you wish to explore the refuge's *northern* lands.

With the directions provided in these pages, however, you can walk an interesting, well-defined route through the *southeast* quarter of the refuge, with an opportunity to observe fine spruce, cedar, and hemlock woodlands and lots of active bird life. In addition to hiking opportunities, Sunkhaze provides cross-country skiing and snowshoe ground in winter, canoeing on the main stream, and birdwatching year-round.

Given the limited number of developed trails at Sunkhaze and the refuge's remoteness, hikers should definitely carry the map and trail directions in this book with them. Carrying a USGS quad is advisable, too, and hikers are well advised to bring a compass along while in this refuge. The hike described here is quite well marked, but other routes in the refuge are not so.

Hikers also should be aware that hunting is allowed in the refuge during certain weeks of the year. For current use conditions, contact the Refuge Manager, Sunkhaze Meadows National Wildlife Refuge, 1168 Maine Street (US Route 2), Old Town, ME 04468-2023. Telephone 207-827-6138 or visit the Web site at www.fws.gov/northeast/me/snk.htm.

To reach the trailhead for this hike, turn off US 2 onto County Road on the east side of the Penobscot in Milford. This road is paved and winds through a residential area, crossing meandering Otter Stream three times. Continue eastward as the road becomes gravel, crosses over Baker Brook, and runs more northeastward. Going over Little Birch and Birch Streams, the road comes in a few minutes to the well-marked trailhead on the north side of the road. A trailboard with information stands here, and there is adequate parking for seven or eight cars. (There are *two* points of access to this hike. Enter via the *easternmost* of the two, as described.)

The Johnson Brook Trail can be walked in various directions, but here we describe a loop that takes the hiker to all the most interesting spots in this section of Sunkhaze Meadows Refuge. Walk north on a grassy woods road from the trailhead through mixed-growth woodlands dominated by spruce and white pine. Sweet fern and low shrubs border the trail as you move northward, and you are likely to see some of the 200 bird species that frequent the refuge. The road is broad and open in most places, and makes an excellent snowshoe or Nordic skiing route in winter.

You soon pass a side trail on the left. You'll emerge here on the return side of the loop. Continuing north, you also pass an open corridor in the foliage to the left and right. Bird counts are taken periodically from measured points on this bird transect to monitor avian life in the refuge. Nearly 0.5 miles into the woods, you come to another, marked trail junction. Keep right here and walk about 0.25 miles to an interesting beaver flowage dotted with standing dry-ki. Water is trapped here and other similar places by beaver activity. If you sit quietly here in early morning or evening, you may see a variety of birds and other fauna.

Next, retrace your steps to the last trail junction, where you turn northwest and right, moving into the middle ground of this hike. The trail, still an undulating tote road, moves through mixed-growth forest dominated by spruce cover. The route bears southwestward 0.25 miles from the last junction and narrows to a winding path over a stretch of low ground. You traverse three sections of boardwalk now, a helpful assist in spring in this area of sometimes low, sodden ground.

The spruce cover yields at a broad junction shortly. Turn right and northwest for a short side trip to acreage probably once farmed in this remote corner. Passing over another boardwalk, you'll find stands of birch here and other deciduous growth favored by deer and snowshoe hares in season. An old foundation is visible also.

Returning to the trail junction, continue straight ahead and south through wooded, low ground, passing a trail to the right, which leads to open areas that have been "hydroaxed" to inhibit the growth of overstory and allow the establishment of understory browse, which favors certain species such as woodcock. Walking south on level ground, you step along four boardwalks in this section, arriving shortly at another marked trail

CEDAR SWAMP

junction. (Watch carefully for this turn. It is easy to miss.)

Go left and northeast on this rougher, narrow trail, which proceeds through patches of blowdowns and wet terrain. The trail winds continuously and, in a section where there are more board-walks, takes you through a splendid cedar swamp. It is shaded here, the densely grown cedars blotting out the light. These trees flourish in this boggy, cool atmosphere and inhibit the growth

BEAVER BOG, SUNKHAZE PRESERVE

of competing species. Dense groves of cedars such as this have become less and less evident in recent decades. The extensive cedar stand seen here is a rare experience.

The trail leaves the cedars, and you walk east over varied cover to the trail junction passed near the beginning of this hike. Go right and south at this junction with the main trail, and walk out to the trailhead over the woods road by which you entered the refuge. The total distance around the main loop, with walks on the side trails to the beaver flowage and, later, out to the abandoned farmstead, is 2.5 miles.

Great Pond Mountain

DISTANCE (ROUND TRIP): 4.25 miles
HIKING TIME: 2 hours, 30 minutes
VERTICAL RISE: 838 feet
MAP: USGS 15' Orland, ME

A part of the Great Pond Mountain Wildlands, administered by the Great Pond Mountain Conservation Trust, this interesting upland gives hikers exceptional observation points over Mount Desert Island, many coastal hills, and the northern Maine coast. Well hidden back in both private and protected woodlands north of US 1 in Orland, Great Pond Mountain provides a relaxed, attractive hike in quiet surroundings amid 4,300 acres of extensively trailed coastal countryside. Assembly and protection of the Wildlands began in 2005, and 2.86 million dollars were raised through private donations to acquire the protected acreage. The mountain is the centerpiece of the more westerly of two major parcels, its summit ledges in private holdings used through the generous permission of the owners. Part of the 875-acre Dead River parcel, the west slope of the mountain is accessed via trails from its southwest near the Craig Brook National Fish Hatchery. The Wildlands feature a variety of terrain, from mountain to marsh, an impressive list of native plants, and interesting bird and animal populations.

To hike the mountain, travel US 1 to a point 1.5 miles east of the junction of US 1 and ME 15 in Orland, 6 miles east of the center of Bucksport. Turn north on a side road signed Craig Brook National Fish Hatchery, and follow this road, which is first paved and then gravel, westward to the hatchery grounds. If this is a first visit, you may wish to spend some time exploring the hatchery grounds before setting out. You are on the site of America's oldest salmon hatchery, established in 1871. The hatchery raceways and display pool may be seen on the hillside, which drops toward Alamoosook Lake. The visitor center provides engaging displays and information on the propagation and research done here.

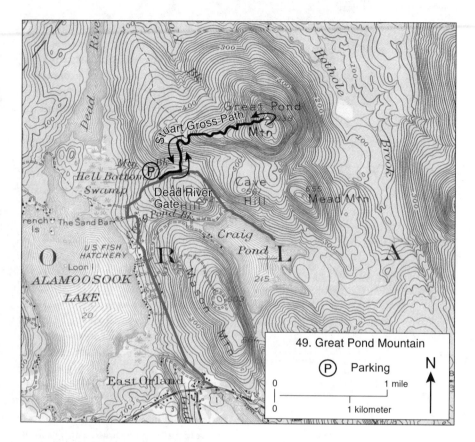

Drive past the hatchery and continue on Don Fish Road (also known as Nature Trails Road) for a half mile to Dead River Gate, where there is parking. The hike begins here at the gate as you walk about 0.4 miles northeast to the trailhead on Don Fish Road. Watch on the left for a sign indicating the Stuart Gross Path. Walk left into the woods on this trail. Here you head north on easy grades in young hardwoods for 0.3 miles. You next descend slightly and arrive at a junction with the Mountain Trail, where you turn southeast and then northeast, rising soon toward Great Pond's summit. Land here and off to the northwest appears to have been cut over in logging operations 20 to 30 years ago, perhaps more. Follow the trail east as it climbs

onto more mountainous terrain, running over exposed ledge and fractured granodiorite as you go higher. The path ascends on the bed of a former tote road and the track is evident in the scanty topsoil. Views begin to open up back to the west and south as you ascend the 1.1 mile length of the Mountain Trail. Behind you are occasional outlooks over the Dead River and Alamoosook Lake. Deciduous growth gives way to white pine, balsam, red spruce, and pitch pine as you get nearer the 1,038-foot summit plateau, continuing always eastward.

Cresting Great Pond's top, the mountain's most striking views are suddenly before you. Some of the lower hills of Hancock County are to the east and southeast, including Mead Mountain

RIDGE TRAIL AT GREAT POND MOUNTAIN

(south), Oak Hill (southeast), Flag Mountain (east), and Flying Moose Mountain (northeast). Off to the far southeast lies Mount Desert Island with the numerous low peaks of Acadia National Park, and, beyond it, Swans Island, Frenchboro, and the Cranberry Isles. To the east of Acadia you will spy Frenchman Bay and the Schoodic Peninsula. One could reasonably argue that this is the finest broad view of Penobscot Bay waters, islands, and uplands available anywhere on the Maine coast, with the possible exception of those seen from Ocean Lookout in the Camden Hills (see Hike 14). Choose a clear day to hike here, as this exceptional perspective shouldn't be missed.

The summit can seem rather indefinite on this mountain. It's very much worth walking around and exploring amid the scrub. If you hike beyond the flat, open spaces that offer the excellent views noted, and continue into the low scrub to the north, you'll find the true, wooded summit a couple of hundred yards farther on.

When you're ready to head down, find the Mountain Trail again and descend on it west, keeping left at the bottom of the west slope, then bearing south and left on the Stuart Gross Path. Retrace your steps on the Gross Path out to Don Fish Road and bear right for the short walk back to the Dead River Gate parking area.

50

Black Point Brook Loop, Cutler Coastal Trail

DISTANCE (AROUND CIRCUIT): 5.8 miles

HIKING TIME: 4 hours

VERTICAL RISE: 400 feet

MAPS: USGS 7.5' Cutler, ME

Away "downeast" lies a hikers' preserve that will delight anyone drawn to those precincts where land and ocean merge dramatically. The Cutler Coastal Trail offers a demanding, interesting, and truly spectacular tramp along eastern Maine's border with the Atlantic, providing hikers with access to ocean views rivaling those of California's Big Sur. Great sea cliffs, rolling surf, unspoiled heathlands, and constantly varying terrain are all a part of this quiet and little-visited route.

The Cutler Coastal Trail is also an excellent example of cooperative efforts among government agencies, preservation organizations, and conservation teams to protect a key natural area and to adapt it sensitively for recreational use. The property was acquired by Land for Maine's Future and developed with the guidance of the Bureau of Public Lands in the Maine Department of Conservation. Construction of the Cutler Coastal Trail has involved the efforts of the College Conservation Corps of Maine, the Maine Conservation Corps, the Maine Coast Heritage Trust, wildlife biologists, recreation specialists, and regional foresters. The result is the longest coastal trail in Maine and, certainly, one of the most beautiful on the Eastern Seaboard.

This route is described as a loop day-hike of 5.8 miles. For those who wish to complete an overnighter or longer in these woods, it is possible to extend your walk to a second loop that leads to primitive campsites at or near spectacular Fairy Head. The longer double loop is 9.8 miles in length, offering a long walk above the coastal cliffs, and an opportunity to camp above the ocean, with a return via a trail that bisects the preserve's wooded inland.

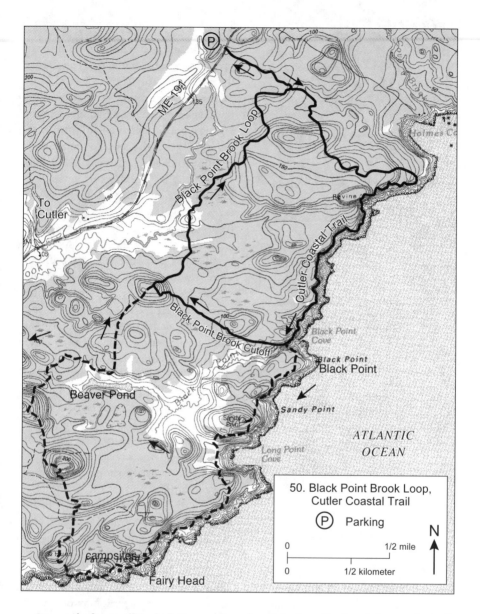

To reach the trailhead, drive south from US 1 in Machias on ME 191 to the village of Cutler. Staying on ME 191, drive 3.8 miles north of the Cutler post office, and locate the trail marker on your right at the edge of an attractive heath. When you've found the trailhead, drive another 100 yards farther north and park in a small gravel lot on the right-hand side of the road. Walk back to the trailhead when you're ready to hike.

From the trail signboard, the path runs across the heath, eventually dividing 4 miles inward, with one route heading around to the southwest, and the other–the one you'll follow–heading more or less straight southeastward through the woods. The path runs along a nearly obliterated Jeep track in the tall grass. Entering the woods on what shortly becomes a grown-up old tote road, the blue-blazed trail meanders generally eastward through stands of red and white spruce and northern white cedar. Eye-catching patches of green *Sphagnum centrale* and *Sphagnum gergen-sonii* are interlaced with equally abundant plots of haircap moss. Clumps of rhodora and ground blueberries lie on both sides of the path. You arrive at the first trail junction 0.4 miles in from the paved road. (You will come back through this junction on the return.)

The trail is easily followed through dense growth to the east-northeast. Open spots interrupt the close-grown cover from time to time. Stands of birch and alder grow amid the dominant white spruce. You will soon reach a long, straight corridor, at the end of which brush blocks the road; bear right on the blue-blazed trail to the southeast. After turning, you pass the first of several cedar groves in this section of the hike and walk through a clearing. Patches of reindeer lichen grow here and there.

The trail wanders southeast and south through a dense white spruce bog and passes two low granite outcrops. You will also pass some older, taller stands of trees. Farther along, you come to another broad cedar grove traversed by a boardwalk. Unharvested cedar bogs of this type are increasingly rare, and it's worth a stop here to take in this exceptional forest. The trail now works its way continuously southeast and south through more spruce, birch, and balsam, intersects with other tote

CUTLER HARBOR

roads, and eventually arrives, running eastward, in more open terrain occupied by sumac growth. You'll hear the sound of the ocean soon and emerge, in a few more minutes, on the cliffs high above the Atlantic.

The superb outlooks here are just the first of dozens that exist along the next 2 miles as the trail follows the clifftops southwestward. The trail climbs northwest to reach higher ground, then pulls around to your left to cling to the heights above the cliffs once again. You walk over uneven terrain, with the trail climbing onto a higher vantage point one minute and then dropping closer to the surf the next. Cutting inland momentarily, the trail will quickly reverse itself and cross some high, vertiginous spots over the ledges. You'll probably never gain or lose more than 50 feet of elevation in any one part of this precipice walk, but the cumulative effect of so much up and down work is rather like climbing an 800-foot hill before day's end.

Warning: The route in this section skirts a series of plunging cliffs. Use great caution, especially in wet weather.

Working your way southward, you skirt several coves, cross some grassy heathland, and clamber over fractured seaward ledge before reaching Black Point. Here there are impressive outlooks back northeast to the headlands along which you just walked. Those wishing to walk to Fairy Head will continue south at this junction above Black Head and, later, Long Point Cove. Those walking the Black Point Brook Loop will turn right and west at this junction.

The Black Point Brook Cutoff leaves these spectacular cliffs and leads to an interesting walk into the interior. Traveling west and northwest, the return

trail gradually progresses inland over several rock ribs, rising gently but steadily through scattered hardwoods. There are good views across the heath in many places. At 0.8 miles from the cliffs, you reach a trail junction where the Inland Trail from Fairy Head comes in on your left. Go *right* and northeast at this junction.

Meandering for a while through tall swale, the trail often dips in and out of more stands of the area's characteristic white spruce and pulls steadily northward. Blue blazes on ledgy outcrops mark the route, which crosses seasonal arms of Schooner Brook. The trail here is well groomed and easy to follow. Traversing a series of small grassy or wooded hummocks, the path pulls continually to the northeast, crosses the open heath, and arrives at the trail junction with the Coastal Trail once again. Turn left and northwest at this junction for the 0.4-mile stroll out to the road. Walk the paved road northeast the short distance to your car.

Safety note: Hikers who bring children with them on any part of this route should be aware that the author's references to unprotected precipices high over ledge and open ocean are not exaggerated. For the careless, the danger of long falls onto ledge or into deep waters with treacherous currents is real. This hike is one of the most beautiful of its kind in eastern North America, but all trail users should walk with caution when near the cliffs. Hikers should also carry plenty of drinking water on this hike.

Hikers seeking more information about low-impact camping possibilities here should contact the Maine Bureau of Public Lands, State House Station 22, Augusta 04333. You may also consult the Maine Department of Conservation's Web site at www. maine.gov.

To make this an overnighter, you can continue to follow the Cutler Coastal Trail beyond its junction with the Black Brook Cutoff and continue above the ocean, past Black Point. Pass several coves and walk south to Fairy Head where there are limited campsites. The return from Fairy Head can be made by retracing your steps to the Black Brook Cutoff where you turn left and west, following the directions given earlier or following the Cutler Costal Trail west and then north, skirting a beaver pond. Including the Fairy Head loop in this hike stretches the total distance to 9.8 miles. Tent spaces at Fairy Head are available on a first-come, first-served basis.

Index